The Book of
Ruth

Andy Lee

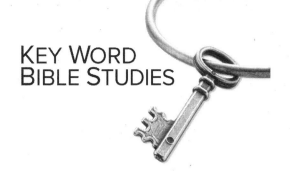

KEY WORD
BIBLE STUDIES

The Book of

Ruth

Andy Lee

*A 31-day Journey
to Hope and Promise*

AMG
PUBLISHERS
ADVANCING THE MINISTRIES
OF THE GOSPEL

Key Word Bible Studies
The Book of Ruth

Published by AMG Publishers. All Rights Reserved.

ISBN: 978-0-89957-519-3
First Printing, 2015

Special thanks to the late James Strong (1822–1894), creator of the *Strong's Exhaustive Concordance* and the Strong's numbering system used extensively in the word study tools published by AMG Publishers that are also featured prominently in this study.

Cover design by Bright Boy Design, Chattanooga, TN

Editing by Rich Cairnes and Rick Steele
Book Design by PerfecType, Nashville, TN

Printed in the United States of America
20 19 18 17 16 15 –RO– 6 5 4 3 2 1

This study is dedicated to my friend,
Pastor Bonnie Beam.
Thank you for sharing *The Key Word Study Bible*.
It changed my life and my ministry.

ACKNOWLEDGMENTS

God gave me a brilliant team to help write and publish this Bible study on Ruth. I must say, thank you. . .

To Rick Steele who championed the idea to write a Bible study based on *The Key Word* the moment I pitched it to him at a writers conference in Florida.

To my agent Blythe Daniel, who advised me to write more heart question throughout the study, not just the last section.

To Trevor Overcash, who agreed to keep my author name "Andy" rather than "Andrea" and allowed my input on the cover.

To Rich Cairnes, my copyeditor, who not only polished the manuscript but challenged some of my commentary and questions which made me dig deeper and in turn write a better, truer, and easier to understand Bible study.

To the women of Wednesday Warriors at Lifepoint Church who patiently ran this marathon with me as I wrote each lesson. Thank you for your input, encouragement, and prayers.

To my sweet family who endured pizza and laundry hamper overflows. Thank you for believing in this call to write. Thank you, Mike Lee, my favorite and only husband, for supporting our family so that I can stay home and write full time.

And to my Jesus. I fell in love with you all over again writing this study. Thank you for being my Redeemer. You know how I need one.

CONTENTS

INTRODUCTION

When we read the Bible our eyes touch an ancient document first written in languages very different from our own. I'll never forget the day I realized that the Bible was not originally written in English. My subconscious knew this truth, but my entire brain hadn't yet comprehended it.

I must give Beth Moore credit for my awakening. As I worked through one of her studies, she incorporated ancient words throughout her commentary. This sparked an incredible hunger inside me to plow beneath the English text. One of my friends attending seminary recommended *The Hebrew-Greek Key Word Study Bible,* published by AMG Publishers. Using this resource changed the way I read and studied my Bible. It began to breathe in my hands. Biblical stories were no longer stale; they took on new life.

This is the purpose of *The Key Word Bible Study Series.* AMG wants to empower you to discover the living, breathing Word—to teach you how to dig beneath the black-and-white print. This study guide is formatted like *The Key Word Study Bible.* Bold numbers next to specific words in the Scripture verses correspond to the Old Testament and New Testament dictionaries printed in the back of the guide. Questions throughout the lessons direct you to the dictionaries, where you'll discover the Hebrew or Greek words and their meanings.

All Scripture is quoted from *The Key Word Study Bible,* English Standard Version, unless otherwise noted. *The Complete Word Study Dictionary* (2 printed volumes, Old Testament and New Testament), another AMG resource, is used for definitions not found in the *Key Word.* Those definitions are noted with "CWSDOT" or "CWSDNT."

The format of this study is unique. Rather than dividing the study into chapters or weeks, there are thirty-one lessons/days. Each lesson can be done in thirty minutes. I know you're busy. It's a perfect study to enrich your quiet time. You can accomplish this study of Ruth in a month individually or divide the study into six or eight weeks for group discussion. Though I love the thought of your individual study, I hope you'll find a group to share Ruth with you.

Each lesson begins with a life story, an introduction to one Hebrew word incorporating its meaning into our modern lives. You might laugh . . . maybe cry, but hopefully as I share my heart you'll know you aren't alone, and you'll begin to understand the word I attempt to define by example.

The lessons end with a prayer employing that ancient word. Praying scriptural prayers is an important precept, but praying the biblical languages unites our prayers with the hearts of the people who penned the holy text. I hope you'll pray them out loud even if you're not in a group. I'm praying with you.

Finally, as you work through the lessons and read my commentary, you'll notice that resources I quote spell Hebrew words differently. This drove me crazy until I found the reason for these discrepancies—our alphabets aren't the same. Again, this was something I knew, but I never considered the implications. We don't have corresponding letters to spell the Hebrew words. So, you may observe spelling and phonetic inconsistencies. None is wrong; each has a basis for its spelling. The process of writing Hebrew words with English letters is called *transliteration,* and it's more an art than a science.

It's my prayer that studying the beloved book of Ruth this way will breathe new life into your Bible study. I pray you feel the Bethlehem dirt on your face, experience the warm harvest night breeze, understand Naomi's bitter desperation, and most of all comprehend Jesus, our Redeemer, our *Gâàl,* and what he did for us as never before.

Day One

An Introduction to Redeemer; More to Come . . .

Gâàl (gaw-al′)

RUTH 4:13–17

I confess. I want to read the end of a novel at the beginning of the book. Sometimes I pester my husband to tell me how a movie ends before it's over—especially if there's a lot of tension or the story is heartbreaking. Some people would ask, "Well, why continue to read or watch if you know the ending?" It's a fair question, but I have a fair answer: I don't want to miss the details of the story, and if I know it ends happy, then I'll persevere through the painful parts to get to the good ending.

Actually, I've just realized it's no different from my husband watching a recorded football game even when he knows the final score. It drives me crazy! But I know he wants to watch every play.

Truth is I never allow myself to read the end of the book, and my husband always refuses to tell me the end of the movie, but the beauty of being an author is that you can start with the end if you want. So, rather than beginning this study of Ruth with the first chapter, let's be bad. Let's start with the last.

Yes, this will take away any suspense, but many of you studying this with me already know the blissful ending. If you are new to the Bible and the book of Ruth, I pray that starting with the ending will help you see the faithfulness of God all the way through every event of this narrative.

Actually, I think it's a perspective we need to keep while living this life. When hardship, disease and sorrow come, we can know how *our* story will end—grief and pain will one day be no more—because we know that Jesus, our Redeemer—our *Gâàl*—lives.

Digging for treasure

Before we start our excavation, I must introduce the characters with a quick summary just in case you aren't familiar with the book of Ruth or you need a refresher:

> **Naomi** *and her husband moved their family from the country of Judah to Moab to survive a famine. Not long after the move her husband died, and her sons married Moabite women. But ten years after their move, both sons died.* **Naomi,** *distraught and desperate, moved back home, and* **Ruth,** *one of her daughters-in-law, followed Naomi back to the land of Judah to help take care of her.* **Ruth** *gleaned wheat in a field to find food for Naomi, and that is when she met* **Boaz,** *the man who would make everything okay* (author's paraphrase).

Now that you know the short of the story, let's dig in.

1. Read Ruth 4:13. Who got married?

I love weddings. They are such happy occasions holding so much promise for two people in love. Ruth and Boaz's wedding was no doubt a joyous occasion, but this matrimony was one of divine purpose and destiny. Hold that thought as we begin to excavate these verses.

2. Read Ruth 4:13. In your own words, describe what God did for Ruth.

". . . and the LORD gave her conception, and she bore a son."

The *New International Version* translates God's gift to Ruth this way: ". . . and the LORD *enabled* her to conceive." The ancient word translated as "gave her conception" or "enabled her to conceive" is the Hebrew word *nāthan*.

3. Read the definition for *nāthan* below from *The Complete Word Study Dictionary Old Testament* and explain the picture formed in your mind when combining this definition with what God did for Ruth.

"A verb meaning 'to give, to place' . . . This Hebrew word also means 'to put, to place, or something literally placed' . . . It could also be something figuratively placed."

What picture does this definition paint?

God not only enabled her to get pregnant, he placed the seed inside. *Nāthan* evokes the imagery of God placing a son inside her womb—his hand giving her this gift. I love this. He's such a personal God. As we dig into the ancient text and study Scripture please remember that every word on the page points to the character of God. The wisdom of God. The love of God.

For Ruth.
For you.
And for me.
For Jews.
And for Gentiles.

It's a big-picture story of salvation, but don't miss the details. Someday when you're in a tough place, you will need to remember how good and faithful God is. Have you experienced his faithfulness, his *hand* in your life? When?

4. Let's witness God's faithfulness to Naomi, too. Read Ruth 4:14. Why are the women giving God praise? What has he done for Naomi?

This is the same Hebrew word used in Ruth 2:20. "And Naomi said to her daughter-in-law, 'May he be blessed by the LORD, whose kindness has not forsaken the living or the dead!' Naomi also said to her, 'The man is a <u>close relative</u>[1350] of ours, one of our redeemers." (ESV)

6. Look up **1350** in the Old Testament Dictionary in the back of this book. Read the definition of *gâàl*. Which meaning relates to the context of this verse?

Stop for a moment. Take a deep breath. The book of Ruth is filled with tangible metaphors of Jesus and what he did for us. I'm praying that our collective and individual need for a big "G" *gâàl* will resonate in deep places, deeper levels of understanding as we study. With this in mind, read the definition again.

We're just getting started. Let's keep going.

7. According to Ruth 4:14, who has been redeemed, Naomi or Ruth?

Actually, they both were redeemed, but the townswomen sing of Naomi as the one who needed a kinsman-redeemer, a *gâal*. It's my hope that as we continue to discover the treasures of this story and unravel its woven tapestry we'll learn the significance of the women's song about Naomi's need for a *gâal*. We'll learn as we read the back-story that this Jewish woman moved with her family to a non-Jewish land, was gone for ten years, and returned to her hometown with nothing. No husband. No sons. No means to survive. Nothing. It's likely that her husband sold or "leased" their land to fund their move.[1] When she returned home destitute, she needed someone to *redeem* her family name and land. Only someone from her husband's family could buy the land in order to keep it in the family—and, in the process, keep *her* in the family. Naomi was not a blood relative of Elimelech's family.

9. Just so we're clear about the meaning of *redeem*, look it up in a dictionary and write the first few definitions—you'll be tempted to skip this because you might have to get up and find the dictionary or your smartphone. But stretching the legs is a good thing. Go find your dictionary. I think you'll be glad you did.

Have you ever redeemed something? What did you need to redeem it? Did it cost you anything?

In order for something to be redeemed, there must be a *way,* or *rules,* as well as a *redeemer* to do the redeeming, and it costs something. For instance, an item must be purchased before a coupon's value is received.

You've read Ruth 4:14 twice already, but three times a charm. The excavation gets even more exciting as we continue to dig. "Then the women said to Naomi, 'Blessed be the LORD, who has not <u>left</u>[7673] you this day without a redeemer, and may his name be renowned in Israel!'" (ESV).

9. Look up **7673** in the Old Testament Dictionary in the back of this book. According to the definition, what does this verb mean? What does this word "most often" express?

If I replace our translation with the literal definition of *shâbath,* the verse reads like this: "Blessed be the Lᴏʀᴅ, who has not *ceased, ended* or *rested . . . gâàl.*"

10. What does this mean to you?

God provided the kinsman-redeemer (the grandson if you read verse 15). But I would like to plant the thought that not only did God not leave Naomi without a *gâàl,* he *never* rested one minute, closed the door, burned the bridge, *ceased* providing the opportunity for Naomi's redemption. And by leaving that door open, God himself was her "bigger picture" *gâàl*—her big "G" *gâàl.* He was the open door. Because he was the Provider, he was the Way for her to be bought back.

He never ceases providing the opportunity for us, either.

Connecting with other Scripture

11. Writing down Scripture helps it stick in our mind and sink deeper into our hearts.

Write John 14:6 and underline the three things Jesus says he is.

12. According to this verse, how do we get to the Father?

13. Read Psalm 103:1–5. According to the psalmist, who redeems his life from the pit?

The Psalms amaze me. As David penned words of praise, he prophesied of Jesus, the Redeemer. Generations later the prophesied One would be born under the stars in a little town called Bethlehem—the very same village where Ruth met Boaz. But Bethlehem is not the only thing the Savior of the world and these simple people have in common. Read Matthew 1:1–6.

14. Who were Obed's parents?

15. Who was Obed's grandson?

16. Whose is the last birth recorded in Matthew's genealogy? (1:16).

17. What did Jesus do for us?

What a family tree! Who would've thought that everyday, normal people, even unholy ones, were ancestors of Jesus? But they were. And two of those ancestors are the main characters of the book of Ruth. Two unlikely, ordinary people living their lives, doing the best they could through drought and famine, heartache and grief. Common people used by God in a big way. It just goes to show . . . you never know what God is going to do.

Some commentaries theorize that the book of Ruth is a fable rather than a true story because of the symbolism running through the book, but if that were so, this lineage wouldn't be recorded in the Gospel of Matthew. The lineage is evidence of the validity of Ruth's life, and this confirms God's hand in our individual lives. He is a personal God. Her story does seem too good to be true. But so does our salvation.

Bringing the treasure home to our hearts

A few years back I was stuck on the word "redeem." I don't know why. I don't remember if I participated in a Bible study about redemption or heard a song about it played on the radio. Maybe a sermon. I can't recall. But I do know that somewhere, somehow, I began to pray for God to redeem my daily mistakes—big and little. I began to live with the peace and assurance that Jesus could and would redeem the painful words that I lashed out at my kids on bad mommy days. I simply prayed, "God, please redeem those words." That prayer has never ceased from my lips. Every mistake, big and little, such as misspelling a literary agent's name, or adopting a puppy even with the likelihood my son's allergies would flare up (which they did), or the huge blunder of hurting a friend's heart, I've watched God redeem. He takes those mistakes and uses them for something good, better, healthier. He's not only redeemed me for eternity—Jesus redeems my every day.

What about you? Do you need to ask God to redeem something? Do you need Jesus to be your *Gâàl*? What do you need redeemed? Maybe it's your life. Maybe it's something that happened today. Write it down.

Let's pray together

"Dear God, we are amazed by your hand in our lives—the little details you so carefully ordain that lead to something so much bigger than us. Thank you for being our *Gâàl* (gaw-aĺ), our Kinsman-Redeemer for eternity, but also for being our daily *Gâàl*. Please open our minds and hearts to understand this concept in deeper ways. Thank you, Jesus. Amen."

I Don't Belong Here

Gûwr (goor)

RUTH 1:1–2

My husband served in the United States Army for twenty-two years. He'd already been in for four years when we married, so *I served* eighteen. Well, not literally, but when you're married to a man in the Army, you do your fair share of serving your country. One way is leaving home and moving all over the world.

Like Sarah I followed my Abraham wherever God told us to go (which we trusted he orchestrated through the Army's chain of command.) Thankfully, we didn't live in tents like Sarah and Abraham. Government housing is really not that bad. But this girl from southwest Oklahoma often found herself *gûwr,* living as a foreigner, at a new duty station. I learned it took years for a place to become home, and some places never felt that way.

I've not considered Oklahoma home for decades. One summer I went back after two years away to help my niece with her newborn and three-year-old daughters. I returned home during the wheat harvest—just like Naomi returning to Bethlehem during a grain harvest. I love this season. As a young girl, it was my favorite time of year because our sleepy farming community woke up. Our population practically doubled and chances for a teenage romance skyrocketed for my older sister and her friends.

The *wheaties* drove into town for the harvest. I would sit in our front yard and wave to them as they drove by. I was only in elementary school, but I was thrilled when a cute wheatie waved and honked his horn. But besides the cute guys in town and the life that harvest brought, I remember how the summer nights smelled sweet as I sat under the stars with my daddy drinking a cold soda out of a glass bottle.

Returning home during harvest reminded me of who I am. I've lived in Texas, Georgia, Kansas, Germany, Massachusetts, and now North Carolina, but going back home reminded me that even after twenty-three years and seven moves, there's still red dirt in my blood.

Each time I return to that sparse, dry, Oklahoma farm country—fields sprinkled with grazing cattle and combines cutting golden wheat, the Dairy Queen filled with cowboys dressed in starched jeans, white straw hats, and silver belt buckles—I'm transformed into that little girl with Laura Ingalls braids who loved riding horses with her Papaw. I'm reminded I'm a cowgirl at heart.

But even though it felt good to go back to Oklahoma where my roots are, it's even better realizing I don't fit there anymore. Truthfully, no place is really home. I'm not sure if it's the number of years away or simply the fact I've been redeemed into the family of God, but there's something inside me that knows I really don't belong anywhere on this earth. I am *gûwr*. But one day I'll really be home. And so will you.

Digging for treasure

1. Read Ruth 1:1. Why did this family move?

2. Where were they from?

3. We referenced this yesterday, but can you think of any important events that happened in Bethlehem? (Read Luke 2:4–7.)

Yes! This family was from the town where Jesus would be born. Though small, this village was an important place. Bethlehem literally means "house of bread."[1] As we will see later in this chapter, the town of Bethlehem was a place where large crops of barley and wheat were harvested. But . . . I can hardly contain myself when I think that Jesus, *The Bread of Life* (John 6:51), was born in this town—Bethlehem's name proved prophetic on so many levels.

God faithfully dropped a trail of *bread* crumbs leading people to Jesus hundreds of years before his birth, years after Naomi re-entered Bethlehem's gates. Let's read about the importance of that prophecy.

4. Read Matthew 2:3–6. How did the Magi know where the baby would be born? Who was the prophet? Hint: If you have a study Bible, look for the Scripture reference indicated by a letter at the beginning or end of verse 6. References are found in the middle column of many study Bibles or at the end of the chapter.

Commentary on Micah 5:2 states,

> "Seven hundred years after the book of Micah was written, this verse was still recognized as a prophecy for the Messiah. The chief priests and scribes quoted it to Herod (Matthew 2:3–6) when they were asked where the Christ was to be born. Jesus' enemies attempted to use it to prove he was not the Messiah because they knew his hometown was Nazareth in Galilee (John 7:41–42). This prophecy reveals that the Messiah is an eternal Being (*from ancient times*)."[2]

5. Let's go back to Ruth 1:1. Where was this family from Bethlehem moving to?

"In the days when the judges ruled there was a famine in the land, and a man of Bethlehem in Judah went to <u>sojourn</u>[1481] in the country of Moab, he and his wife and two sons" (Ruth 1:1).

6. Before we locate the Hebrew word, look up the definition of *sojourn* in a dictionary and write it down.

7. According to the definition of *sojourn,* did Naomi's family plan to stay a long time in Moab?

Now find the bold number next to *sojourn* in Ruth 1:1 (above). Locate this number in the Old Testament Dictionary in the back of this book. Read the entire definition for *gûwr.* Pay close attention to the commentary section of the definition.

8. Why would the author of the book of Ruth employ this word to describe their move?

Perhaps the author chose this word to indicate that Naomi's family not only planned to live temporarily in this new land but also that her family would *live as foreigners.* No commonality. Different religions. No family.

Desperate times call for desperate measures, but moving to Moab showed *a lot* of desperation. Let's learn some more about Moab. Read Genesis 19:30–38.

9. There are strange and painful stories in the Bible, but that one is really hard to read. However, reading this story was necessary because it shows the origin of the country of Moab. Is it a holy origin? Explain.

Though the book of Ruth doesn't refer to it, Scripture reflects tension between Israelites and the Moabites, who lived east of the Dead Sea.[3]

10. Read Deuteronomy 23:3–6. What does verse 6 command?

So . . . it's not a place you want to live, especially if you are Jewish. But this family chose to move there. Have you ever done something you knew down deep was not pleasing to God and could be dangerous? What happened?

Let's dig some more.

11. Read Ruth 1:2. What was Naomi's husband's name?

In biblical times names were thought to describe a person's character and destiny. Elimelech's name meant "God is my king."[4] Is it strange that a man with this name would move to Moab? Why would he move? We know there was a famine, but maybe other reasons gave Elimelech the courage to move to Moab.

12. When did this story take place according to Ruth 1:1?

13. Read Judges 17:6. What does this verse tell us about the time period?

One commentator wrote, "The famine must have been quite severe for Elimelech to move his family there."[5] That's what I was thinking—the conditions must have been *really* bad for a man whose name meant "God is my king" to move his family to a land of people born out of incest. But if Moab's ancestral line wasn't bad enough, one would surely think the fact that they worshipped a false god named Chemosh to whom the Moabites made *human* sacrifices would've deterred Elimelech.[6] But it didn't.

Maybe the author of Ruth (who is unknown) specifically chose the words, ". . . went to sojourn, *live as foreigners,* in the country of Moab" (Ruth 1:1, emphasis mine) to try to explain that Elimelech did not intend for his family to take on the practices and religion of the Moabites. Maybe he justified that their family would be missionaries in this pagan land while finding food and employment. (They did convert one Moabite—Ruth.) I don't know. That is inference on my part. I usually try to find the best in people.

But the Bible is clear that Elimelech moved his family during a period in Israel's history when the Law was taken more as suggestions than commands. And maybe these circumstances freed this godly family to do the unthinkable. Yet I wonder if Elimelech's decision brought shame and disappointment to his heart once he and his family began to settle into Moab and experience how very *gûwr* they were in that place. I wonder if he would've moved his family back much sooner if he hadn't died so quickly. But one thing is certain: they did not belong there.

I hate that feeling—that sinking feeling in the pit of your stomach when you're somewhere you shouldn't be. The older I get, the more I feel that way here on this earth. But maybe that's a good thing.

Connecting with other Scripture

14. Read John 15:18–19. Why does the world often hate followers of Christ?

15. Read Philippians 3:17–21. Where is our citizenship?

16. Is there anything from Philippians 3:17–21 that resonates with your spirit?

Bringing the treasure home to our hearts

Have you felt *gûwr* in a place where you lived? Do you feel that way about this world? How do you cope with this *foreign-ness*?

As I write this lesson, an old hymn has been playing in my mind: "Can't Feel at Home in This World Anymore." Did you grow up singing it? If so, sing a few bars. If not, here's a link to a Web site where you can find it: http://www.oldielyrics.com/lyrics/the_carter_family/cant_feel_at_home_in_this_world_anymore.html. Enjoy, my friends. They don't write 'em like they used to.

Let's pray together

"Dear God, please don't let us get comfortable in this world. As hard as it is, thank you that we are *gûwr* (goor) here. We know we aren't here for long, but we *are* here, so please use us. Redeem our mistakes for your glory. Let us make a difference in this place. Make others around us hungry to know the God we serve. We love you. Thank you, Jesus. Fill us, Holy Spirit. Amen."

Sometimes We Just Have to Go Back

Shûwb (shoob)
RUTH 1:3–7

I do it all the time. I get my car loaded with suitcase, backpack, computer, snacks, water, gum, and GPS. I'm set. I kiss my husband, say goodbye and give hugs to the kids (at least one child tries to make me feel guilty even though they are 22, 20, and 16.) Big production. I head out the door only to get in the car and realize I forgot something. I have to go back inside.

I hate that.

It's embarrassing.

I've already said goodbye.

However, they're used to it because every time we've loaded our family into the van for vacation, we get as far as the main road out of our residential area and someone realizes he or she forgot something. My husband does a U-turn and we drive back home. I always wonder if the neighbors are watching and what they are thinking—especially after the third time into the driveway.

But sometimes you just have to go back.

I've experienced this even with the need to go back to Oklahoma. It seems that through the years God sent me back home at just the right time—either for my needs or someone else's. Sometimes my own homesickness expedited the decision to buy the plane ticket which otherwise might not have been purchased.

One October when we lived in Boston I was compelled to go home to visit my sister because her mother-in-law was dying of stomach cancer. I felt I needed to share the gospel with her, but when I arrived my sister's mother-in-law had already received Christ.

Had I heard God wrong? Did I not need to come? Was I just there to say goodbye? Though glad to be home I wondered why I was there. A few months later, however, the reason for my trip became very evident. I wasn't there for her mother-in-law, who would pass away a few months later, I was there for my sister.

Christy and I had enjoyed a lovely week together. We shopped and watched movies, laughed and reminisced. It was sweet. But the week after I left she became very sick.

They soon learned that what appeared to be pneumonia was actually her second battle with cancer. She'd fought lung cancer two years earlier and had been cancer free for awhile. But the disease returned with a vengeance.

My next visits were spent helping her husband take care of her. Trying to keep hope alive. But as the days wore on she declined quickly. The day I said goodbye, her neck muscles were weakened so badly she could not lift her head. Her eyes faced the floor, and a stroke had stolen much of her speech.

Had God placed into my heart the desire to go home the first time because he graciously wanted to give me one more *good* week with my sister before she got sick?

I will always believe he did.

Many of us don't live close to family anymore. We live in a culture that is constantly moving and changing—climbing the ladder of success. We often feel that if we go backward rather than forward, we're failing. We're embarrassed when the business goes bankrupt or we have to move back in with our parents because we've lost our job or we can't find a job. Circumstances often make us go back. They make us *shûwb*.

But *shûwb*, though sometimes painful, is often necessary. And God has a plan for our return. Just like he did Naomi's return to Bethlehem. He is in the details as well as the big plan. Maybe the story of Ruth will help you if you ever have to return somewhere. Maybe it will help if you need to *shûwb* to God.

Digging for treasure

1. Read Ruth 1:3–5. When did Naomi's sons get married? Before or after their daddy died?

2. Step into Naomi's sandals for a minute. Why do you think she allowed her boys to marry Moabite women?

Have you let your children do something you knew wasn't good for them? Did your mom ever let you do something that wasn't good for you?

My kids are now at the dating age. It's uncharted territory for us, and truthfully, it's a little painful. But it certainly helps when we *like* their chosen sweetheart. Maybe Naomi *liked* these girls. Let's study their names to see if we can find any reason why this Jewish mother would let her sons marry non-Jewish women.

Some commentaries explain that *Orpah* meant "thick neck."[1] It certainly wasn't the prettiest name nor the most flattering, but maybe her neck or "thick hair" was pretty. (I'm hoping for her sake.) Maybe she had a lot of hair when she was born. Who knows why a mother would name her child *Orpah*. Poor girl. (Yes, Oprah's mom tried, but people mispronounced her name regularly, and "Oprah" stuck.)

But one commentary clarified that *Orpah* is interpreted as "back of the neck."[2] I find this interpretation probably the most likely. Orpah was the daughter-in-law who turned back toward Moab. They saw the back of her neck as she walked away.

Either way, Ruth's name was much better. Her name meant "friendship . . . comrade, companion."[3] What a great name! I love the meaning of *Ruth*. She lived up to her name in this story.

Speaking of names, do you like yours? I've struggled with mine for years. I'm really *Andrea*, but somewhere along the way *Andy* stuck. Sometimes I don't feel either one really fits me. I'm looking forward to heaven when Jesus will hand me a white stone with a new name (Revelation 2:17). But until then I'll just stick with Andy and play with people's minds. They're always confused when I'm not the man they were expecting!

Anyway. Back to the point.

Our names are important to us. In biblical times, however, names were thought to be indicators of personality and providence—they were thought to characterize the person. We know that Ruth's name fit her well. Perhaps all that Orpah really had to give was her looks. Regardless of their names, they were definitely *Moabite* women who married into a *Jewish* family. This would cause problems later on. Let's read the Law.

3. Read Deuteronomy 23:3. Who cannot enter into the congregation of the Lord? How long was it forbidden?

4. Read Deuteronomy 23:7–8. What generation born from the Egyptians could enter into the assembly of the Lord?

So, Egyptians (who once mistreated and enslaved the Israelites and had no relation to them) could enter into worship <u>seven</u> generations before the Moabites could. The Moabites must have really made God mad. But though they couldn't worship, it's believed they could marry. Remember, the Moabites were related to the Israelites through Abraham's nephew, Lot. Some commentators theorize that these *marriages* were not forbidden because of the relation between the two groups.[4] But let's find out why the Moabite descendants couldn't *worship* with the Israelites.

5. Read Deuteronomy 23:4–6. Why were the Moabites forbidden to worship with the Israelites?

The Jewish people are God's favorite. He chose them first when he called Abraham. And they are still his chosen. It seems God is revealing this more and more to the Western Gentile church. For thousands of years Christians have considered themselves better than the Jews. But the same God who gave Moses the words to write in Deuteronomy is the one we love today. Perhaps we should take heed of the Moabite's mistake.

Deuteronomy 23:4 states that the Moabites did not assist the Israelites when they asked for help. They also hired Balaam to put a curse on them. We would think the curse itself would've made God mad at the Moabites, but God is the One who controls curses and blessings, so he turned the curse into a blessing for the Israelites. However, he doesn't control human free will—our decision to lend a hand or refuse to help. The Moabites were given the opportunity to help the Israelites, to show *chêsêd,* and they did not. This is key—paramount. It's the tip of the iceberg. We will be learning so much more about *chêsêd,* but we need to move on for now.

Let's go back to Naomi and her sons, who married women whose children—if they had any—would not be allowed to worship in the assembly of the Lord. This is important. Let's find out if they had children.

6. Read Ruth 1:4–5. How long were Mahlon and Chilion married before they died?

Sidenote: Verses 4 and 5 simply say, "They lived there about ten years, and both Mahlon and Chilion died. . . ." Because of the placement of this verse (after the mention of their marriages to Orpah and Ruth) we assume they were married that long. Actually this sentence only tells us that the family lived in Moab ten years—but the length of their marriage isn't clear. One thing is certain, however.

7. Did they have any children?

No children. Children were essential for the family business and name. Famine and infertility were signs that God's hand, his favor, was withdrawn. With no grandchildren Naomi experienced even greater loss than famine and a dead husband. Ruth and Orpah did, too. They both went childless for up to ten years. That's a long time. Maybe each month they hoped for a miracle. Now their hope was dead. Two husbands. Two sons. Dead. And no grandbabies for Naomi. Absolute hopelessness.

I've wondered why this family from Judah stayed in Moab so long. I've wondered why they didn't go back home when Elimelech died. Why did Naomi and her boys stay? Was it shame? Embarrassment? Why didn't they go back? Why did they marry Moabite women? Why not go back to Bethlehem and marry women there? Was it because there the famine continued? Even if it did, wouldn't it be better to be home with your people—relatives and friends suffering and trusting Jehovah together—than in a place like Moab where God was not worshipped at all?

The Bible does not give answers to those questions. But I think it's good to ask God questions as we study. I think he likes it when we ask. Though I have no divine answers, I do think this family must have gotten used to Moab. Maybe Moab became home for Mahlon and Kilion. I know how hard it is to move kids when they have friends and like their home. Maybe they got comfortable there—a place they didn't belong. But it will become clear in our Day 6 lesson that even if the boys felt at home in Moab, Naomi continued to practice her faith in God. She continued to live *gûwr*. Maybe this is why she did finally decide to go back home.

8. Read Ruth 1:6–7. When did Naomi decide to go back to Bethlehem?

9. Who was going with her in verses 6 and 7?

Both daughters-in-law were going to return to Bethlehem with Naomi at this point. The Hebrew word translated as "return" has layers of meaning I want us to uncover.

"So she set out from the place where she was with her two daughters-in-law, and they went on the way to return⁷⁷²⁵ to the land of Judah" (Ruth 1:7).

Locate the number next to *return* in verse 7 and find its Hebrew counterpart in the Old Testament Dictionary in the back of this book. Answer questions 10 through 12 according to the second paragraph of the definition.

10. What does this verb *mean*?

11. How many times is this verb used in the Bible? Does it have different *shades* of meaning?

12. How is this verb used metaphorically?

In the simplest sense, *shûwb* means "to turn or return." Interestingly, *shûwb* is used in the Old Testament time and time again to describe turning from idolatry back to God—his people's part of his covenant with them. This word described repentance.

Naomi was going home, returning from a land of people who did not worship her God. God gave promises to his people when they returned to him, but the promises we receive because of Christ are even sweeter. Let's look at the old and new covenants.

Connecting with other Scripture

13. Read Deuteronomy 30:1–3. According to these verses, when would God restore the Israelites' blessings?

". . . and return[7725] to the LORD your God . . ." What is the Hebrew word?

It seems Naomi was finally heading in the right direction.

The Deuteronomy passage above reveals God's covenantal blessing to his people, Israel. It was a covenant that offered blessings and warned of curses for those who disobeyed. But we now live on this side of the cross.

14. Read Galatians 3:10–14.

• How did Christ redeem us? (v. 13)

• How was he our *Gâàl*?

• What do we receive by faith?

Rather than the physical blessings promised to the Israelites in the first covenant, now we are promised the Holy Spirit. We're assured more than blessings. We are guaranteed the Spirit of Jesus himself living in us. That's better than a two-story home with a white picket fence and two and a half children any day. Houses need repair, fences have to be painted, children grow up and move away, but the Spirit of Jesus leads us, fills us, loves us, and promises never to leave us.

Have you experienced his Spirit? In what ways has the Spirit helped, counseled, comforted, spoke to, or guided you?

Bringing the treasure home to our hearts

Has there ever been a time when you were going the wrong direction in life or found yourself in a place where you didn't belong? What did you do?

Maybe you're in a place like that now—a place you don't want to be, but you see no way out. Please hear me. THERE IS ALWAYS A WAY OUT. THERE IS ALWAYS A PATH BACK TO JESUS. There's a good chance the Holy Spirit has been prompting you. He's probably also put somebody in your life leading you back to him. *Shûwb*. He's waiting.

Let's pray together

"Dear Father God, some of us know the pain Naomi knew. We live in places we don't want to be in. We endure heartache and grief. We're desperate. There is nowhere to go but back to you. Help us *shûwb* (shoob). We ask you to forgive us. We repent of our sin. We renounce our distrust of you. Help us live by faith not by sight as we return home. And Lord, some of us pray this prayer for those we love who need to come back to you. Holy Spirit, prompt them to *shûwb*. Oh, may they *shûwb*! May they turn back to you and be filled with your Spirit. Thank you, Jesus. Amen."

Love Is a Verb

Chêsêd (kheh´-sed)
RUTH 1:8–10

What shall I do? I expect to pass through this world but once. Therefore any good work, kindness, or service I can render to any person or animal, let me do it now. Let me not neglect or delay to do it, for I will not pass this way again. ~ an old Quaker saying

We met in church. Her clothes were dirty, hair a mess, and it was difficult to understand her when she spoke. My heart went out to her. Yet I admit I was a little wary. I'd been taken advantage of before.

Despite my fears, I began greeting her every Sunday. One day she told me it was her birthday, so the next week I brought her a present. Maybe that's what started the phone calls. I don't remember how I got involved, but now she frequently calls asking for a ride to the grocery, and while we shop she asks me to buy some of the items she's placed in the basket. The food she chooses isn't always the basics nor cheap, but I buy them when I can. Yet I confess I don't always do so with grace because I wonder if I'm being conned.

This happened the other day when she called asking, or slightly demanding, that I run an errand. It was easier to go to the store without her because of her physical problems, yet I knew this would mean paying for the entire purchase. Extra cash in my wallet and the feeling I should help her prompted my decision to oblige, but I was fighting a nagging question . . . *Am I being conned?* Despite the negative thought, I drove to the store with her list in hand.

I hadn't voiced my concern to anyone, even to God, but he knew. Driving home from delivering her groceries, a voice on the radio teaching a brief lesson between songs said, "It is better to give and be *conned* than not to give and worry about being *conned*."

There is nothing like a tangible answer from God.

The teacher on the radio used the same words I'd just asked myself—that nagging thought running through my mind. I couldn't believe my ears. There was absolutely no doubt I had done the right thing by helping this woman, and the nagging voice of reason was silenced.

I realized that the decision of whether to give is not mine to make. I'm called to give what I can, but the integrity of the one asking for help is not mine to judge.

The truth is: I've never felt bad about helping someone, to give *chêsêd*, but I grieve the opportunities I've not seized—those passed by because I questioned the person's integrity.

Digging for treasure

1. Read Ruth 1:8. Naomi experienced a change of heart. What did Naomi tell Orpah and Ruth? How did she hope the Lord would deal with these women?

"May the Lord deal kindly[2617] with you, as you have dealt with the dead and with me" (Ruth 1:8).

2. Find **2617** in the Old Testament Dictionary in the back of this study. What is the significance of this word? Does "kindly" sufficiently translate the meaning of *chêsêd*?

3. According to the definition, which psalm best describes this Hebrew word, and how many times is *chêsêd* used in this psalm?

4. Look up Psalm 136 and find how many verses are in it.

5. The psalmist repeats *chêsêd* in every verse. What does this signify?

6 According to the psalmist, how long does God's *chêsêd* ("mercy" or "love," depending on your Bible translation) endure?

7. Give the simplest definition of *mercy* according to your favorite dictionary.

Does *chêsêd* mean more than *mercy*?

8. Look back to the definition of *chêsêd*. What other words does this "masculine noun" indicate?

9. What character quality do these words have in common? Or perhaps a better question: What feeling do these words evoke inside of you as you read them out loud?

It's hard to find just one word. In fact, we don't have one English counterpart which does the Hebrew word justice. We need many words to explain *chêsêd*. How differently Psalm 136 would read if translators used the different words that define *chêsêd* rather than repeating only one aspect of this word throughout. In order to grasp a fuller picture of *chêsêd*, let's swap out some words:

> "¹ Give thanks to the LORD, for he is good, for his <u>kindness</u> endures forever."
>
> "² Give thanks to the God of gods, for his <u>lovingkindness</u> endures forever."
>
> "³ Give thanks to the Lord of lords, for his <u>goodness</u> endures forever."

10. Your turn. Write out Psalm 136:4–6, replacing what your Bible used with one of the other words that describe *chêsêd*. (You listed these words in question 8.) Once you've rewritten these verses, read the example verses (1–3) above and yours aloud. How does this change your view of God's *chêsêd*?

Let that sit with you for a moment. What does it mean for us to have a God who will always help us—a God whose "DNA" is kindness?

11. According to Micah 6:8, what does the Lord require of us?

Can you guess the Hebrew counterpart for *mercy* or *kindness* in Micah 6:8? Yes, it is *chêsêd*.

12. According to this verse, does God require us to give *chêsêd*?

Chêsêd is love with hands and feet. It involves more action than feeling. That's why the translation of "love" for *chêsêd* can throw us off. Our view of love shades the meaning.

And my *chêsêd* and your *chêsêd* could never match God's. His *chêsêd* never tires. We definitely need his Holy Spirit to help us.

Chêsêd is who God is and what he requires of his people. This is why he was so angry when the Moabites refused to help the Israelites after they fled Egypt. They knew better. They were related! But maybe more importantly, the God who extends *chêsêd* to us expects us to do the same for others—especially his people. Can you think of a time when you extended *chêsêd* to someone? Can you think of a time when you extended *chêsêd* to someone Jewish?

Let's get back to the story and see how these biblical characters demonstrated *chêsêd*.

13. How have Orpah and Ruth shown *chêsêd* to their dead husbands?

14. How have they shown *chêsêd* to Naomi?

15. Read Ruth 1:9. How is Naomi demonstrating *chêsêd* to her daughters-in-law?

16. What is their response?

I think this is a beautiful scene—not very graceful or pretty but beautiful none the less, because it demonstrates how much both Orpah and Ruth loved Naomi. They loved their Jewish mother-in-law, who taught them about the Jewish God. I picture them huddled together, clinging to one another, tears pouring as they grieve over yet another goodbye. They don't want to leave her, and they're not trying to hide their feelings or grief. Let's dig into this verse to better paint the picture.

17. The *New International Version* reads, "Then she kissed them and they wept *aloud*. . ." (v. 9b). The *English Standard Version* reads, "Then she kissed them and they *lifted up* their voices and wept." Were these three women weeping quietly? How would you describe this scene?

They weren't just crying. Their hearts were breaking as they lifted up their souls in grief. Wailing. Most of us have experienced these tears—the ones you can't keep silent. I longed so badly to be from another culture as I silenced loud sorrow buried deep in my chest during my sister's wake. I felt I would explode. But by God's grace, for my family's sake, I held it in. How I wanted to lift up my soul with noise. You can bet I did so when I was alone. Have you experienced this grief? What were the circumstances?

18. Once they regained their ability to speak, what did Orpah and Ruth tell Naomi in Ruth 1:10?

19. Go back for a moment to Ruth 1:7. Where are these ladies when Naomi stops to tell them to go back home?

They had already left Moab! Their bags had been packed. They were out of their residential area, on the main road leading out of town, perhaps on the highway already out of town, when Naomi had a change of heart. She told the girls to make a U-turn without her—to *shûwb*.

I don't know if it was despair, *chêsêd,* or shame that caused her change of heart. I'm sure that returning to Bethlehem with Moabite girls could be humiliating. She'd already lost so much. Maybe going home with them would bring even more heartache. But maybe she really was granting them *chêsêd*, granting them freedom. I'm choosing to believe the best again. I believe she was granting them *chêsêd* by releasing them from their marital duties, which bound them to her.

Connecting with other Scripture

Jesus also taught of *chêsêd*. I got so excited the first time I found the Scripture reference to this verse in Matthew. It was a light bulb moment for me. I hope it is for you, too.

20. Read Matthew 9:10–13. What assignment does Jesus give the Pharisees?

"... I desire mercy[1656], and not sacrifice. ..."

Remember, the New Testament ancient manuscripts from which our English Bibles were translated were written in Greek and the Old Testament manuscripts were Hebrew. The word "mercy" in this verse was translated from the Greek word *eleos.*

21. Locate **1656** in the New Testament Dictionary in the back of this study. Summarize the definition of *eleos.*

22. What Hebrew word holds similar qualities of *eleos?*

Many believe that the first manuscripts of the gospels were written in Hebrew and later translated to Greek—the manuscripts used for our translations. Whether or not Matthew was written in Hebrew or Greek, Jesus spoke Hebrew or Aramaic. There is a very good chance he told the Pharisees he desired "*chêsêd* not sacrifice."

The commentary below by Spiros Zodhiates explains the significant relation between these two words:

> ". . . *eleos* is heavily influenced by its use in the Septuagint as an equivalent of *chêsêd*, mercy, lovingkindness, which referred to acts of covenant loyalty, expressions of kindness arising from the obligation of a relationship. *Eleos* is used of acts of divine intervention, especially in fulfillment of the promise of salvation, as displays of God's covenant love. . . . <u>Loyalty and love for Yahweh were measured in the manner and quality of one's dealings with others.</u> To be hardhearted, letter-of-the-law insistent, and unmoved by any extenuating circumstances violated the spirit of the Mosaic Code. In fact, mercy was characteristic of God's treatment of His people, and therefore was commended to them as the social ethic which He expected them to follow."[1]

As stated above, "To be unmoved by extenuating circumstances *violated* the spirit of the Mosaic Code—violated! That's a strong word. Jesus taught *chêsêd*. He **was** *chêsêd*. Time and time again he told the religious, the dogmatic, that they were missing the point.

23. In Matthew 9:10–13, Jesus is quoting Hosea 6:6. Read this Old Testament prophecy. What does God desire?

This word has been translated from *chêsêd*. As Jesus taught the Pharisees, he led them back to the prophets of old. He not only told them they were missing the heart of God, he himself demonstrated *chêsêd* over and over.

Bringing the treasure home to our hearts

Has anyone shown you *chêsêd*? What's your story?

Does this lesson tug at your heart and encourage you to help others in need? Explain.

Let's pray together

"Oh, God, help us! We are born with a sinful, selfish nature. One of the first words out of our mouths is 'Mine!' We live in a mean and dangerous world—some people take advantage of those helping them. Please remove fear and selfishness from our hearts so we can graciously extend *chêsêd* (kheh´-sed). We love you. We want to serve you. We want to be people of *chêsêd* (kheh´-sed). Thank you, Jesus, that your Holy Spirit is in us. Transform our hearts. Amen."

The Kiss of Respect

Nâshaq (naw-shak)
RUTH 1:11–14

I cannot tell people goodbye. You'd think I'd be pretty good at it after our many military moves. But when it's time to give our farewells I never actually say the word. I usually say something such as, "See you soon!" or "Take care!"

When I was hugging my sister goodbye for the last time here on this earth, I refused to say the "g" word. I somehow managed to look into her baby blue eyes despite her inability to lift her head. (Maybe God gave her the strength to look up. It seems he did, though the memory is fuzzy.) We stared into each other's eyes, tears halted for a brief moment, and I said, "I *will* see you again." I've never said anything with such conviction and determination.

My sister worked as an elementary school teacher for thirty years. Her teacher eyes could burn a hole through you if she willed. I didn't teach school quite that long, but I have the same gift. If anyone had snapped a photo in that incredible, gut-wrenching moment, it would've revealed tangible faith. Our eyes spoke dogged determination that this was not a forever goodbye but more like, "See you tomorrow." I could feel our faith.

I don't think Orpah liked saying the "g" word, either. Rather than a locked stare between her and Naomi, she said goodbye with a *nǎshaq*—a kiss that expressed more than words.

Do you hate saying the "g" word? What do you do or say to acknowledge the farewell?

Digging for treasure

1. Read Ruth 1:11–14. Why did Naomi command Ruth and Orpah to return to their families?

2. How does your Bible translate the last sentence in Ruth 1:13? If it's the same as one of the translations below, put a star next to it. If yours is different, write it here.

- "... It is more bitter for me than for you, because the LORD's hand has gone out against me!" (NIV)

- "... No, my daughters, for it is exceedingly bitter to me for your sake that the hand of the LORD has gone out against me." (ESV)

- "... it grieveth me much for your sakes that the hand of the LORD is gone out against me." (KJV)

This is why it's good to study different translations. You've heard the saying, "Don't put all your eggs in one basket." Well, I think the translations above demonstrate how Bible verses can be translated and interpreted differently. Even learned theologians with letters after their name translate and interpret Scripture with human eyes. Honestly, I believe that the translator's perspective of Naomi reflects the translator's interpretation.

Until writing this study, I only read this verse out of my *New International Version* and interpreted it as Naomi considering her loss more bitter than Ruth's and Orpah's. But now I'm not so sure. Which translation seems more correct to you? Which do you think reveals Naomi's heart?

Regardless of Naomi's heart, whether she felt this situation was more bitter for her or she felt it was more bitter for her daughters-in-law, one thing is not in question—the reason for their tragedy. Naomi is convinced that God's judgment has done this. The word "bitter" holds the key to understanding her words.

I know bitter. I experienced bitterness when Christy died. And I didn't like experiencing it. It was uncomfortable because I had loved God since I could remember, but I was angry and disenchanted with faith and prayer. The first time reading the book of Ruth, I read Naomi's words of bitterness with my own grief filters. I understood her feelings that the Lord's hand was against her—or at least I thought I did. But Naomi's words mean much more than my 21st-century American eyes see. I can easily interpret her words through my own grief, but we must dig into the Hebrew to fully understand her bitterness and why she viewed her loss as more bitter (if we agree with the New International Version's rendering of this verse).

The Hebrew word translated as "bitter" is *mar*. The definition of *mar* is "bitter (both literally and figuratively); sad, fierce, violent. Denotes the heart-crushing experience of family turmoil, sterility, impending death, discontent, an unfulfilled death wish, personal suffering and hardship . . . and the Lord's judgment upon believers."[1]

3. *Mar* denoted tragedy, but according to the definition, whose judgment did it indicate? Against whom?

So, maybe Naomi wasn't being dramatic or insensitive to Orpah's and Ruth's loss. Remember, these women were Moabites. Pure Jewish blood didn't pump through their veins. If we consider the *English Standard* or *King James Version* more correct, we understand that Naomi felt even worse because her sin had caused this suffering that her daughters-in-law endured. Let's read more about God's judgment.

4. Read Zephaniah 1:14–15. What will the cry on the day of the Lord be?

". . . the sound of the day of the Lord is <u>bitter.</u>[4751]"

5. Look up **4751** in the Old Testament Dictionary in the back of this study and write down what you discover. What's the Hebrew word?

Bitter. This is the same Hebrew word Naomi used to describe her state. Naomi's choice of words declared God's wrath on her (or at least what she believed was the cause of her pain.)

6. Describe the day of the Lord according to Zephaniah 1:15.

Dark days. Before you get upset about God's judgment and wrath, read Zephaniah 2:1–3 and discover the hope for those who seek the Lord.

7. Who will be sheltered or hidden?

That's Naomi's God doing the sheltering. That's our God. He always promised his people they could return to him.

8. Read Psalm 57:1. Where does the psalmist find shelter?

I love this Scripture verse. It evokes feelings of safety and security in my spirit. We will visit this Scripture again in the study. Hold on to the thought of God's *shelter* or *covering*, but for now we must get back to the three ladies wailing in the middle of a dusty road. But hopefully, studying the Scripture in the book of Zephaniah assists your understanding of Naomi's words. Her bitterness wasn't just because she was mad at God. She believed she was under God's wrath because of her family's move to Moab . . . yet she was returning home.

9. Read Ruth 1:14. What did Orpah do?

Translators often use several English words to adequately translate the meaning of a Hebrew word. That is the case in this verse in the *New International Version*. "Kissed goodbye" are the words used to translate *nâshaq*. The *English Standard Version* simply writes, "Then Orpah kissed her mother-in-law . . ."

The definition of *nâshaq* is "to kiss. Kissing signified the payment of homage or true love. Conquered people kissed their conquerors to show their submission . . . Sometimes *nāšshaq* denoted respect."[2]

10. What did *nâshaq* sometimes denote?

Respect. This word jumped off the page as I studied the definition. I think it human nature for us to think less of Orpah because she chose to travel home rather than stay with Naomi. Her name alone didn't indicate much character, so she appeared weak. Some theologians have interpreted her name as "stiff-necked" because she didn't turn toward Naomi's God. But what if she was the girl who always obeyed the rules? What if her decision was one made out of *respect* for her mother-in-law's wishes rather than Orpah's lack of love or tenacity? Granted, her kiss is her farewell, but I think it was more. I think it proves her love for Naomi and her respect for her mother-in-law's wisdom.

Have you made a decision based on respect for someone? Have you ever regretted it? If so, why?

Naomi faced the consequences of her family's sinful move to Moab. Though her sorrow was bitter, she chose to *shûwb*. Remember, *shûwb* means "to turn around," but it also means "to repent." Though Naomi was grief-stricken and believed that the Lord's hand was against her in judgment, she never disavowed her faith or her God.

We don't like to think of God's wrath or judgment. It's much more pleasant to focus on his grace. But the truth is: his grace wouldn't be needed if it weren't for his judgment. He is a holy and righteous God who from the very beginning of time created us to live with him. That was his purpose. His plan. He doesn't want religion. He wants relationship—a relationship that fills, transforms, and makes eternal beings. But there is a catch. We must realize and recognize our sin, our need for a Savior. When we acknowledge and repent of our sin, we are asking Jesus to be our Savior and to fill us with himself.

Connecting with other Scripture

11. Read Romans 2:1–11.

* What will happen to those who are self-seeking?

* Who will receive glory, honor, and peace?

* What group of people will be the first to be judged?

- Who will be the second group to be judged?

12. What does this tell you about Jew and Gentile? Are the Jews still set apart from the Gentiles in the eyes of God?

Some of you may be thinking, "Um-m-m . . . but what about Galatians 3:28?" I'm so glad you asked! Galatians 3:26–28 reads, ". . . for in Christ Jesus you are all are sons of God, through faith. For as many of you were baptized into Christ have put on Christ. There is neither Jew nor Greek, there is neither slave nor free, there is no male nor female, for you are all one in Christ."

Scripture is God-breathed and does not contradict itself. When Bible verses seem to contradict each other, study! So . . . we're going to study.

I remember learning an academic concept called "replacement theology." That term simply meant that since Jesus died for all of us, we all became "Jews," replacing his chosen people with believing Gentiles and believing Jews. But this is not correct theology. Yes, we who are baptized in Christ, both Jews and Gentiles, are clothed in him. When God looks at us in the Spirit, there is no differentiation, even male or female. But *apart from Christ* the Jews are still God's people. They are still the ones chosen first and judged first.

13. According to Romans 2:4, what do some "presume" (ESV) or "show contempt" (NIV) against?

14. What leads us to repentance?

Sometimes bad things happen simply because we live in a fallen world. Sometimes bad things happen because God is trying to get our attention. But every time something bad happens we can trust that God has good purposes.

After harboring anger against God for a few months after my sister's death, I decided I had a choice. I could choose to live angry with God, believing the worst of him— that he was a heartless, wrathful, angry God in the sky—or I could choose to stand on his goodness. I repented of my anger and disillusionment, and asked for greater faith. I then began to walk daily again with determination to believe that God is always good. Peace and joy replaced my anger.

15. Read Romans 8:28. Who makes all things work for good and for whom does he make all these things work?

This has been one of my favorite verses for a long time. I know I won't see "the good" of some heartbreaks until heaven, but I must believe this verse. Even though there are a few things I'm not able to see God's good in yet, there are many things I have seen him make work for good. Some of those things were worked out for good in my life, some in friends' and family's lives. And there are hundreds of stories in the Bible testifying to Romans 8:28. Naomi's story is one of them.

Bringing the treasure home to our hearts

Has God worked through difficult circumstances in your life, making them good? Please share your story here. It's good to write down what he has done.

Let's pray together

"God, thank you for your kindness, which leads us to repentance. Use whatever it takes in this life to make us more like Jesus and ready for your judgment. We look forward to the day when we will bow before you and *nâshaq* (naw-shak) our Savior's nail-scarred feet. We love you."

Your God Will Be Mine

Ĕlohîym (el-o-heem)

RUTH 1:15–18

will never date one of those guys, much less marry one!"

Famous last words.

I know better than to say *never.* Yet this word jumped out of my mouth before I could lasso it back. My proclamation was a knee-jerk rebuttal to a prediction.

"I'll give you two years before some Army guy sweeps you off your feet and carries you all over the world," the superintendent hiring me prophesied.

About a year after his statement I found myself going to coffee with a tall, dark, and handsome soldier. It wasn't an official date, just coffee with friends. I don't know what came over me, but as we drove to the coffee shop I daringly asked, "How long do you plan to serve in the Army?"

"Twenty years . . . would that be a problem?" he replied, turning the question on me.

Would that be a problem?

This wasn't a date. This was coffee with friends. We hadn't officially been on a date yet. Why would he ask such a question? (But, then, why would *I* ask the question I had asked?)

I couldn't believe my own ears as I heard myself say, "No! No . . . um . . . that would be okay."

Funny how love changes things. Faith does, too. Combined they are unstoppable.

Months after our ride to the coffee shop, Mike asked me out on a real date. That night he was baptized. As our small church group huddled in prayer, he prayed, "Lord, thank you for showing me your will and allowing me to follow it."

Now my soldier was not only tall, dark, and handsome, but he trusted the same God, *'Elohiym*, whom I followed. I would've married him that night.

Digging for Treasure

1. Read Ruth 1:15. To whom is Orpah going back?

2. What does Naomi urge Ruth to do?

3. Read Ruth 1:16. What is Ruth's response?

This is probably one of the most loved Scripture verses in the Bible. Many couples use it during their wedding ceremony. Ruth's words reveal commitment not only to stay with her mother-in-law, but to exchange her whole life—family, nationality, and faith—for Naomi's.

Have you ever given up everything—culture, religion, family—for someone else? What motivated you?

4. What do you think motivated Ruth to make this statement?

Ruth proclaimed, ". . . Your people shall be my people, your <u>God</u>[430] my God" (Ruth 1:16).

5. Who were Ruth's people and who was her God? (Look back to Day 1.)

Ruth does not refer to Naomi's God with a little "g."

6. Locate **430** in the Old Testament Dictionary in the back of this study. Write down the Hebrew word and how it's pronounced. Read through the definition and summarize what seems most important.

7. Is this word singular or plural? (I think this is amazing when you consider the Trinity.)

Read Genesis 1:1. This is the same Hebrew word for "God" as the one Ruth used.

8. What did ʾĔlohîym do?

"*Elohiym* is the Hebrew word for God that appears in the very first sentence of the Bible. When we pray to *Elohiym,* we remember that he is the one who began it all, creating the heavens and the earth and separating light from darkness, water from dry land, night from day."[1]

When Ruth announced that Naomi's God, *Ĕlohîym,* would be hers, she was claiming faith in the Hebrew God. The one true God. Naomi had lost everything, but she hadn't lost her faith in *Ĕlohîym.* Ruth's statement proves that though Naomi lived in Moab, she never bowed to Chemosh; she never stopped believing in her God—the maker of heaven and earth. I find it interesting that Ruth would choose to believe in a God whom Naomi proclaimed to be the cause of her suffering and bitterness, but this was an accepted view of all gods during these ancient days:

> "The culture in the cradle of civilization lived with a pantheon of gods who themselves existed in a kind of hierarchy. There were gods of war, fertility, and harvest who were acknowledged by the culture as a whole, and under these, a litany of household gods, usually statues made of crafted wood, clay, and precious metals, that were placed on the family mantel. People related to each of these gods by means of specific rituals and ceremonies whereby their protection and favor could be gained. Each family literally 'owned' their own god . . . When the living God of the Old Testament came along, he seemed to fit right in with this way of thinking, describing himself as the God of Abraham, Isaac, and Jacob. He gave Moses a regimen of laws, rituals, and ceremonies to be followed . . ."[2]

9. Why do you think Ruth clung to Naomi, denying her own gods and family?

Ruth promised to claim Naomi's God as hers, but as she continued to proclaim her faithfulness to her mother-in-law, her words revealed she already knew Naomi's God.

10. Read Ruth 1:17. From whom will Ruth expect discipline if anything but death separates them?

"The LORD" was translated from the Hebrew name, YWHW or *Yᵉhōwāh*—to the Jewish people, a sacred name that refers to his saving power.

> "The word refers to the proper name of the God of Israel, particularly the name by which He revealed Himself to Moses (Exodus 6:2–3). The divine name has traditionally not been pronounced; primarily out of respect for its sacredness . . . it was written without vowels in the Hebrew text of the Old Testament, being rendered as YWHW. However, since that time, the vowels of another word, *adonay* (H136), have been supplied in hopes of reconstruction of the pronunciation . . ." (CWSDOT)

I love studying the names of God. We've just learned three of them:

• *Ĕlohîym* (el-o-heem)

• *Yᵉhōwāh* (ye-ho-vaw)

• *Adonay* (a-do-naí)

Ruth incorporated two of them in her proclamation: "Your people shall be my people, and your God (*Ĕlohîym*) my God. Where you die, I will die, and there will I be buried. May the LORD (*Yᵉhōwāh*) do so to me and more also if anything but death parts me from you" (Ruth 1:16 –17).

A book that I keep on my shelf for both reference and devotional reading is *Praying the Names of God,* by Ann Spangler. In reference to YWHW, Spangler writes,

> "After the destruction of the temple in A.D. 70, the name was not pronounced. *Adonay* was substituted for *Yahweh* whenever it appeared in biblical text. Because of this, the correct pronunciation of this name was eventually lost. English editions of the Bible usually translate *Adonay* as "Lord" and *Yahweh* as "LORD."[3]

11. How does your Bible translation spell the word "Lord" in Ruth 1:17? If it is all caps, which name of God is she referring to?

Lᴏʀᴅ—*YWHW* is associated with the name linked to what God did for the Jewish nation when he freed them from slavery. He freed them with power and might.

Lord—*Adonay* implies a master/servant relationship.

So, Ruth spoke the name of Naomi's God as if he were already hers. She not only recognized the Jewish God as the Creator, *Ĕlohîym,* but also the redeeming, saving, covenant God, *Yᵉhōwāh.* She would later come to know the Lord (Master) of her life, *Adonay.*

It's an interesting progression. First, recognizing the one true God who created all, then acknowledging his redemptive powers and plan, and finally coming to know him as the Master of your life.

In what phase of this three-part progression do you find yourself?

Let's get back to Ruth.

12. Read Ruth 1:18. When did Naomi stop urging Ruth to go back home?

The *English Standard Version* simply says that Naomi surrendered the fight when she realized how "determined" Ruth was. But read the definition of the Hebrew word from *The Complete Word Study Dictionary Old Testament:*

Āmaṣ: "a verb meaning to be strong, determined, bold, courageous; conquer."

Ruth was:

- Determined

- Strong

- Courageous

- Bold

. . . and I can't fight the feeling that she was *desperate*.

She didn't want to go back home to her family and her gods, as she had found something good, precious, true, powerful. Naomi and her *Ĕlohîym* were like no relationship Ruth knew growing up in Moab. Despite Naomi's current bitter, grief-stricken attitude, Ruth experienced the strong, joyous, faith-filled Naomi before the death of her sons.

Once you've tasted the love of *Ĕlohîym*, you can't go back. I believe Ruth was a good woman; her character provided resilience and fortitude to take care of her mother-in-law once they arrived in Bethlehem. However, her determination to stay with Naomi proves more than goodness to me—it proves *desperate love*. She had stumbled on a treasure, and she was not letting go.

Connecting with other Scripture

Jesus once told a parable about a man who also found a very special treasure—it was a pearl.

13. Read Matthew 13:45–46. What did the merchant do when he discovered the pearl?

14. How do you interpret this parable?

Commentaries explain that the kingdom of heaven is so wonderful and glorious that a person would sacrifice everything to gain it. Was that your answer? If so, you stand with some of the great commentators of all time.

But what if we have the meaning of the parable flipped?

Listen to a testimony I once heard from a lady named Mary:

> "I lived a crazy life. A very broken life. I searched for love in all the wrong places and ended up in a cult. But by the grace of God I escaped that place of darkness and found a church that preached the love of Jesus. Before I knew Jesus' love I always thought that the parable of the beautiful pearl was about Jesus being the pearl and me the merchant, but now I know that I had the meaning of the parable turned around. Jesus is the merchant who sold everything for me, and I am the beautiful pearl."

Does her story resonate within you? It does in me. I think Mary was right. How I pray for all of us to understand how much the Lord loves us! Let's see what Jesus sold to redeem us.

15. Read John 1:1–5. To whom was John referring as the "Word"?

16. What did the "Word" do? Does this remind you of a Hebrew term for God that we have studied today?

"In the beginning was the Word[3056], and the Word was with God and the Word was God." (John 1:1)

17. Look up **3056** in the New Testament Dictionary in the back of this study. What is its simplest meaning? What does it mean in reference to Christ? (Note the third part of the definition.)

The Greek counterpart (remember, we are in the New Testament) for "Word" is the term *Logos.* This ancient term does mean "word" but the Greeks also used it when they referred to "the governing power behind all things."[4]

Let that sink in for a moment. John is claiming that "the governing power behind all things" left his heavenly throne to pour himself into skin, be born under the stars, and die a criminal's death.

18. What did Jesus give away to "buy" us?

Why would he do that?

19. Read John 3:16. Why did God, *Ĕlohîym, Yᵉhōwāh, Adonay,* give his Son up for sacrifice?

Bringing the treasure home to our hearts

Do you have trouble believing/knowing/trusting that Jesus loves you?

Some of us struggle trying to comprehend Jesus' love for us. We find it hard to get that knowledge past our heads into our hearts. Maybe if there were a Ruth in our lives who was ready to leave everything she knew to take care of us, then we could begin to understand Jesus. Maybe if we had a daddy who never left, or a mom who wasn't always finding fault.

We don't have to live in the maybes. What has been done is done. *Adonay, Ĕlohîym, Yᵉhōwāh, Logos,* lives beyond time. He sacrificed everything for you and me. And he's even more determined, strong, and courageous than Ruth. He won't let go.

Like Naomi, we need to give in. Stop the fight. Let him walk with us, take care of us, and love us.

Let's pray together

"*Ĕlohîym* (el-o-heem), you alone are worthy of our praise. You alone are worthy of our worship. We acknowledge you as our God today. We acknowledge Jesus as our Savior, who gave it all for us. We pray you take this knowledge from our heads to our hearts. Let us overflow with your love. Make us desperate for you. Strong. Courageous. Determined. We'll follow you anywhere you lead. We love you. Amen."

Day 7

The Power and Goodness of God

Shadday (shad-dah´-ee)

RUTH 1:19–22

I was twenty-two years old. Fresh out of college, ready to take on the world, and I found myself debating once again with my dad about faith in Jesus.

This was not an unusual scene. We had sparred over religion consistently since junior high. Dad had attended church when I was young, but somewhere along the years he became interested in the New Age movement, and we debated our beliefs often.

But tonight was different. Actually, it was just like the other debates with my dad. I couldn't persuade him to believe. But on this night, I questioned if *I* were right. I concluded that if I couldn't convince him, I was wrong. I trusted my dad's conclusions over my convictions even though I *knew* Jesus.

After our debate I threw up my hands in frustration, and these words marched past my lips: "Fine! I will try believing like he does. God is the god of all religions. They are all the same."

The silence that followed my proclamation took up residence in my soul. I've never experienced such darkness. At the time I didn't realize what I had done.

Years later I would understand that my proclamation denied Jesus as Savior of the world. His Spirit slipped out the back door of my heart.

I walked into the debate full but crawled out empty.

But *Shadday* never gave up on me. The Almighty was faithful to lead me back to him. Looking back, I'm so thankful for the void and that nothing could fill it but Jesus.

Digging for treasure

1. Read Ruth 1:19. Explain how the town reacted when Naomi and Ruth entered Bethlehem.

". . . the whole town was <u>stirred</u>[1949] because of them."

"Stirred" has been translated from *hûwm.*

2. Locate **1949** in the Old Testament Dictionary in the back of this book. How does the definition change your idea of Bethlehem's reaction to these two women?

3. How long had Naomi been gone from Bethlehem?

4. What could've caused the townspeople's reaction? Why were they unsure it was Naomi and disturbed by her presence?

Have you had this happen to you? You've been shocked by a friend's appearance or friends were shocked over your change? What happened?

5. Let's read Naomi's response to their shock and gawk. What name does she tell the women to call her and why? (Ruth 1:20)

"Do not call me Naomi, call me <u>Mara</u>[4755]. . ."

6. Explain the meaning of *Mara* from the Old Testament Dictionary in the back of this book.

I'm thinking Naomi looked rough. Perhaps she was dressed in black from head to toe. Downcast. Pale. Dark circles under her eyes. Maybe her hair was tangled. Her clothes torn. She was mourning. In this moment in time she couldn't imagine that anything good could or would come out of this. Her feelings were so strong, not only were they evident by her appearance, she solidified them with a name change. Naomi's name meant "pleasantness and delight," but she had definitely lost her pleasantness.

Grief is like that. It seems so permanent at the time. I remember after my sister's death watching a young couple come out of the movie theatre laughing and holding hands. As I watched them through my mourning eyes, the fog of grief so thick it colored my perception and thoughts, I actually wondered if I would ever laugh like that again.

7. Whom does Naomi blame for her "permanent" emptiness and her return? What does she say he has done?

". . . for the <u>Almighty</u>[7706] has dealt very bitterly with me."

8. Find **7706** in the Old Testament Dictionary in the back of this study. What Hebrew name for God was Naomi using? How many times does this word occur in the Bible, and how many times is it found in the book of Job?

9. According to the definition, to whom did God appear and identify himself with this name when the man was ninety-nine years old?

10. If this name is used in the book of Job thirty-one of the forty-eight times it appears in the Bible, and God identifies himself with this name when he promises Isaac's birth the following year, what can you conclude about the power of this name?

11. Do you believe God, *Shadday,* brought this misfortune on Naomi?

12. Do you think she felt abandoned by God? Have you ever felt abandoned? Explain.

13. Read Ruth 1:21. Ruth said she went away full, but now she has returned empty. Grief causes a void. Is there anything good about being empty?

Does God cause suffering and heartache? We want to say no! It's unconceivable that a good God would make people suffer.

He is sovereign yet we have free will. So, many times our own decisions cause our pain. I wonder if Naomi was tempted to be angry with Elimelech; the move was his idea. I'd probably blame my husband. Unfortunately, I can also empathize with Naomi's God-blame, and I know all too well the feeling that God is punishing you. I also know the emptiness accompanied by sorrow. Grief clouds our ability to see hope. But the author of Ruth didn't want to leave the readers in despair at the end of the first chapter. Naomi's soul was as empty as her stomach, but when you're empty, you can be filled. Oh, what a difference a day, week, month, or year can make!

14. Read Ruth 1:22. What is the glimmer of hope?

Connecting with other Scripture

15. Read John 10:10. Why has the thief come, and why has Jesus come?

"I came that they may have life and have it abundantly[4053]."

16. Identify the Greek word in the New Testament Dictionary in the back of this book, number **4053**. Read through the definitions and list the words other than "abundantly" that stand out to you.

The meanings of this Greek word according to Strong's Dictionary include:

· Abundance

· Advantage

- Anything More
- In Abundance
- Out of the Ordinary
- Beyond Measure.[1]

Jesus was saying, "I have come so that they may have an *advantage, an out-of-the-ordinary, beyond measure, superfluous, overflowing* . . . life.

17. Do you think that the abundant, or *out-of-the-ordinary,* life Jesus was referring to meant that our lives would be problem-free? Explain your thoughts.

18. Read Romans 5:1–5. How have we been justified?

19. How do we have peace with God?

20. What do believers rejoice in?

21. What does:

- Suffering produce?

- Perseverance produce?

• Character produce?

22. What has God poured into our hearts? How?

Love changes things.

Bringing the treasure home to our hearts

Life changes us whether we want it to or not. Pain, grief, sorrow, and disappointment are part of life. How have you changed during the last ten years? Do you feel you've changed for the better or worse?

If you've changed for the better, what made you better?

If you've changed for the worse, what caused your decline?

No matter where we are today, better or worse than ten years ago, we can't change the past—but we can change the future. Though Naomi was bitter believing God's hand forced her loss, she never stopped trusting the integrity of the one true God and chose to return home, the place of her faith. She could've spent the rest of her days in Moab living empty and mad at God.

I know empty. Although waves of grief have washed over me, nothing caused Dark Empty like the loss of Jesus in my life. While that year without Jesus proved dangerous and lonely, my faith grew muscles on steroids when I acknowledged him as my Savior again.

Let's pray together

"*Shadday* (shad-dah´-ee), we love you! Forgive us our sins. Help us return home to you. Fill us with Jesus. We want to be *out-of-the-ordinary* people, changed by your love. If our countenance is sorrowful, help us exchange our grief for trust so hope may replace the shadows of bitterness with the light of joy. Amen."

Day 8

Destiny

Miqreh (mik-reh´)

RUTH 2:1–3

Our townhomes were separated by a house in between, but the three yards behind the houses were joined by one fence. This made one big yard that allowed our children to run back and forth between our back doors—even early on Saturday mornings. I can still picture my friend's son's face smashed against our glass door trying to see if we were awake. And I still remember the grace needed when living so closely together.

Though my husband's military rank would not have normally afforded such a large home, the lack of available post housing ushered us into this beautiful town-house snuggled in the heart of German wine country in the quaint village of Bosenheim. The best part about this living situation was our neighbors. Both Germans and Americans, military and civilian, surrounded us. We could walk to the bäckerei (bakery) a few blocks away where the aroma of fresh brötchen (bread) filled the air every morning, and every harvest the unique smell of grapes fermenting greeted our noses. I was living a dream.

This is where I met a woman who became one of my dearest friends. At the time, she was fighting depression, loneliness, and wounds in her marriage. There were days when she didn't want to get out of bed. There were days when it was hard to be her friend—she probably felt the same way about me, but we were connected by something much stronger than the fence surrounding our yards or the beauty of the vineyards around us.

God had orchestrated our living position. It was *miqreh*.

We've held each other's hearts through grief and joy. She stood by me in spirit and through phone calls as my sister battled cancer and lost the fight. She acted the catalyst for my visits to Israel and Costa Rica—two life-changing trips. And through the years I've stood by her side and counseled her through marital ups and downs and life-changing decisions.

Though now separated by many miles, we've been prayer warriors for one another throughout the last fifteen years. *Miqreh* brought us together, but faith glued our hearts for life.

Digging for Treasure

1. Read Ruth 2:1. Who was Boaz?

2. Describe his character according to your Bible translation.

The English Standard Version describes Boaz as a "worthy man."[2428]

The New International Version introduces him as a "man of standing."

And the King James Version calls him a "mighty man of wealth."

3. Identify the Hebrew word found in the Old Testament Dictionary in the back of this study at **2428**. List some of the uses of this word. What is the "basic idea" of this masculine noun?

4. With the knowledge of the different uses of *chayil,* how would you describe Boaz now? Is he more than "worthy" or "wealthy"?

Maybe I've seen too many movies, but Boaz is looking pretty good in my imagination. He enters the scene in slow motion. (Cue fog machine, spotlight behind him obscuring his face, and suspenseful music.) As he gets closer I see massive, tan muscles, handsome yet weathered features, and a team of mighty men following close behind. And topping all of that, which would make any girl swoon, he is wealthy. Prince Charming has been introduced, though he has not made his grand entrance yet. But there is more to Boaz than meets the eye. Let's find out a little bit about his family.

5. Read Matthew 1:5. Who were Boaz's parents?

Let's refresh our memory about Salmon and Rahab. They have a very interesting story.

6. Read Joshua 2:1–21. Who was Rahab? What did she do for the Israelites?

7. Read Joshua 2:12–14 again. Circle the word repeated several times in those verses.

> "'Now then, please swear to me by the LORD that, as I have dealt kindly with you, you also will deal kindly with my father's house and give me a sure sign that you will save alive my father and mother, my brothers and sisters. . . .' And the men said to her, 'Our life for yours even to death! If you do not tell this business of ours, then when the LORD gives us the land we will deal kindly and faithfully with you" (Joshua 2:12–14).

8. Can you guess what Hebrew word was translated as "kindly?" (Look back to Day 4.)

Yes, Rahab showed *chêsêd* to the Israelites as they did to her. Boaz's mother's kindness continued to the next generation in her son. His mother was a woman of *chêsêd*. She was also a foreigner who believed in foreign gods until she saw the power of the God of Israel. Keep this in mind as we watch this story of love and redemption unfold.

9. Read Ruth 2:2. What did Ruth want to do for Naomi?

10. What was Naomi's response? Did she have hope yet?

11. Read Leviticus 19:9 and explain what God commanded the farmers concerning harvest.

12. Where does Ruth plan to glean? (Ruth 2:2)

13. Whose field does she glean in?

> "So she set out and went and gleaned in the field after the reapers, and she happened to come to the part of the field belonging to Boaz, who was of the clan of Elimelech" (Ruth 2:3).

"Happened" was translated from the Hebrew word *miqreh*. Its meanings include "happened by chance, fate, and destiny" (CWSDOT).

This is my kind of story. It started out painful, but it's getting better fast. The author of Ruth introduced us to Prince Charming (Boaz) and then told us that destiny led Ruth to his field. It's hard for us to imagine her just "happening into a field" with our American eyes. Where I grew up, many farmers lived on their land. The homestead staked their land. But that's not what the biblical farming looked like. I envision it much like the farmland and villages of Europe. Rather than individual farms and homesteads, the farmers lived in villages surrounded by the collective farmers' fields. One ran into the other. Perhaps this was how Ruth found herself in the "part of the field" belonging to Boaz. She couldn't have planned or timed it better if she'd tried.

Have you ever experienced such timing or destiny? Please share.

Connecting with other Scripture

As I write this lesson, the faces of friends who are struggling continue to flash through my mind. Life threw them one too many curveballs. Prayers for healing and provision have not been answered as hoped. So, the story of Ruth is a little Pollyanna, *pie-in-the-sky*, unrealistic. But I think we can learn from Ruth and her actions.

Though destiny seemed to play a major role in Ruth's life, I believe that her faith in the Lord, the same faith that glued her to Naomi, prepared her heart to be led by God into Boaz's field.

One of my favorite Scripture promises is found in Psalm 37. I especially love the translation of these verses in the *Complete Jewish Bible* (CJB). Listen . . .

"Trust in *Adonai*, and do good; settle in the land, and feed on faithfulness. Then you will delight yourself in *Adonai*, and he will give you your heart's desires." (Psalm 37:3–4)

14. According to the psalmist, what four things must be done before you can delight yourself in the Lord and receive the desires of your heart?

15. Has Ruth demonstrated any of these characteristics? Which ones?

16. Read Isaiah 48:17. What does your Redeemer do?

17. Read 2 Thessalonians 3:3–5 and answer the questions:

- How is the Lord faithful? What does he do?

- What does Paul pray for the people?

"May the Lord direct your hearts to the love of God and to the steadfastness of Christ" (2 Thessalonians 3:5).

It's necessary to study the word "steadfastness" in the Greek to fully understand what Paul was saying. The ancient word is *hupomonē*. Read this excerpt from *The Complete Word Study Dictionary New Testament* (CWSDNT).

> *Hupomonē:* "to persevere, remain under. A bearing up under, patience, endurance as to things or circumstances. This is in contrast to *makrothumía* (G3115), longsuffering or endurance toward people. *Hupomonē* is associated with hope (1 Thessalonians 1:3) and refers to

that quality of character which does not allow one to surrender to circumstances or succumb under trial."

18. What is *hupomonē* associated with?

Simply put, Paul prayed for the people to know God's love and experience the hope found only in Jesus.

The other day as I backed out of my driveway, negative thoughts bombarded my mind.

"You're a bad neighbor . . . wife . . . mom . . . friend . . ."

I stopped my car and put it into drive. As the tires rolled forward, the weight of the accusations immediately lifted when the Lord's response drifted through my spirit:

"I don't see you that way at all."

I love when soul-whispers restore my thoughts.

It is true. I could be better at being me, and you could be better at being you, but God doesn't judge us by our works, though he has given us good works to do. He judges us by our faith in Jesus as our Savior.

I always recognize "God-whispers" because they lighten my heart. Satan's accusations and my own fault-finding weigh me down. God's words bring freedom, joy, and a deeper level of understanding of his love and Jesus' sacrifice.

Bringing the treasure home to our hearts

Ruth made a choice the day she decided to walk to Bethlehem with Naomi. On that day she decided to trust Naomi's God as her own.

have a hard time trusting God? Do you believe he has a good destiny planned for you? Why or why not?

Let's pray together

Oh, Lord, help us trust you deeper, more assuredly, every moment of every day. Direct our steps. Guide our ways. Lead us to the right field. Help us do our part, and trust you to do yours. We love you. Thank you for the hope we have because of Jesus. Thank you for our *miqreh* (mik-reh´) in you. Amen.

Day 9

A Blessing

Bârak (baw-rak´)

RUTH 2:4–7

When you ask a native German if they speak English, and they reply, "little," that means they can carry on a conversation. But my *little* of the German language was limited to counting to ten, saying "thank you" and "you're welcome," and greeting someone with "How are you?"

I quickly learned when Germans asked if I spoke their language, my answer needed to be, "Nein." (No). I knew enough of the language to get me in trouble. But unfortunately, that didn't stop me from employing my limited knowledge from time to time.

Most of the Germans I met spoke English, but the older population didn't. One day as an elderly woman made her daily stroll down the street in front of our townhome, I couldn't resist speaking to her. I loved her beautiful, wrinkled face and shining eyes. I knew her walk always ended in the cemetery behind our neighborhood, across from a wheat field. So, though my language skills weren't even nominal, I greeted her as she walked by. *"Wie geht's?"* I asked.

83

Her eyes brightened at my greeting, and she began to tell me in German how she was doing. I didn't know if what she spoke was good news or bad, if I should smile or look concerned.

So, I attempted another German word accompanied with sign language (of which I also have a limited knowledge). I pointed to her face and signed "beautiful" while saying, "Shön." She looked at me with doubtful eyes.

"Yes," I nodded, my eyes locking hers. I pointed to her again and attempted my compliment a second time. She studied me as if she weren't sure how to proceed. A warm smile spread across her tired face and she replied, "Danke." She thanked me as she continued her stroll.

I hope my greeting, though awkward and limited, blessed her. I pray my words were a *bârak*.

Digging for treasure

1. Before we start digging, summarize Ruth's story up to this point. Just for fun, write your summary as if you were Ruth. Remember, you haven't met Boaz yet, you don't even know who he is.

Now to the digging.

2. Read Ruth 2:4–7. Had Boaz been working in the fields all day? Where had he come from?

If he came from Bethlehem, that means he made a special trip to check on his harvesters.

3. How does he greet the harvesters?

4. How do they respond?

5. What does their reciprocal greeting tell you about their relationship? Do they like their boss?

6. What does Boaz's greeting tell you about him?

A long time ago, before commentaries were available at our fingertips via computer/ Internet and apps, my husband ordered *The Old and New Testament Bethany Parallel Commentaries*. These volumes compare side by side the works of Matthew Henry; Jamieson, Fausset, and Brown; and Adam Clarke. The books are gigantic. I just weighed one of them—seven pounds!

The blurb on the front cover boasts, "A complete new concept, allowing the reader to compare the views of three respected commentaries, all in one handy volume." What was *handy* then is simply *heavy* now, but I still lug these dinosaurs (one at a time) off my bookshelf when I need insight. I chuckled when I read Adam Clarke's *Commentary on the Whole Bible* regarding the verbal exchange between Boaz and the harvesters: "This salutation between Boaz and his reapers is worthy of particular regard; he said, 'Jehovah be with you!' They said, 'May Jehovah bless thee!' Can a pious mind read these godly salutations without wishing for a return of those simple primitive times?"[1]

I guess my mind isn't pious because I view those simple primitive times as hard. They are dusty, dirty, famine-laden, dangerous days—at least compared with the year 2014 in America. But Boaz's greeting and his workers' response do reveal another aspect of this man's character.

He's a good one. He's not only wealthy and strong . . . he's kind. He's godly.

The meaning of the greeting seems obvious, but let's finds what happens when the Lord is *with* the people in the Bible.

Read Judges 6:11–16.

7. What did "the LORD is with you" imply to Gideon?

8. Why did Gideon not believe God was with him?

9. What did God promise his presence would do for Gideon?

The Lord's presence promised victory and freedom. Perhaps by his greeting, "The LORD be with you!" Boaz was reminding his workers of the presence and favor of God. The harvest, the end of the famine, surely was evidence of God's presence.

The harvesters' response? "The LORD bless[1288] you."

10. Look up **1288** in the Old Testament Dictionary in the back of this book. From what part of the body is this word derived? When did God use this verb?

11. Look up *bless* in the dictionary. Write down some of the definitions.

12. How does the world envision the blessings of God? Is your view the same? Explain.

"God loves me." I hear these words coming out of my mouth when good things happen. I'm guilty. When circumstances are good, it's easy to feel God's presence and his favor, but not so much when times get hard. Sometimes frustration, discouragement, or grief makes it impossible for me to feel the presence or love of God.

Connecting with other Scripture

13. Read Matthew 5:1–11. Who did Jesus say was blessed?

"Blessed[3107] are the poor in spirit, for theirs is the kingdom of heaven." (Matthew 5:3)

14. Locate **3017** in the New Testament Dictionary in the back of this book and list some of its definitions.

This is a simple understanding of the word, but it holds a deeper meaning that goes beyond the term *happy*. Underline the New Testament meaning of *makarios* according to this commentary by Spiros Zodhiates:

> "The Greek word translated "blessed" is *makarioi* which means to be 'fully satisfied.' In Classical Greek, the word referred to a state of blessedness in the hereafter. In the New Testament, however, the term is used of the joy that comes from salvation. This satisfying joy is not the result of favorable circumstances in life, but comes only from being indwelt with Christ. Therefore, *makarioi* denotes far more than 'happy,' which is derived from the English word 'hap' and connected with luck or favorable circumstances."[2]

15. Explain the difference between the Classical Greek and the New Testament understanding of *makarioi*.

16. How does the meaning of *makarios*, whether experienced in the afterlife or in this life, differ from our understanding of *blessed*?

17. According to Zodhiates, what is needed to be *makarios?*

When Boaz's servants greeted him with a blessing, theirs was probably a wish for blessings of health, wealth, and favor of God. But when Jesus came, the blessings bestowed became more than that which this temporary world offers.

Bringing the treasure home to our heart

Are you blessed by Christ speaking of the blessing . . . *fully satisfied?* If not, what can you do?

Honestly, I'm not always fully satisfied. As I walked into Target the other day to, as Joyce Meyer calls it, *minister to my emotions* (a-hem—shop), this thought lingered in my mind: *As long as I live in this world, I may not be fully satisfied.* We're constantly bombarded with what the world says will fill our longing. It's usually shiny or pretty but the *fill* is always momentary.

I know the passing thought in my mind was not truth because there have been moments in this life when I've soaked in the presence and love of Jesus. During those extraordinary hours, I knew that nothing else was needed. I was full.

Today I've thanked God for the less-than-full moments because they remind me that only something eternal can fill the caverns within. All other blessings are temporary. And that makes me even more desperate to *spend time* with Jesus, *trust* God, *live* this life, *do* good, and *feed* on his faithfulness.

Let's pray together

Jesus, please forgive us when we try to fill the caverns within with anything but you. Thank you that nothing else can *fully satisfy*. Fill us with your Holy Spirit. We pray every day for more of your Spirit. Less of us . . . more of you. You alone *makarios* (mak-ar´-ee-os) us. Amen.

A Favored Foreigner

Nokriy (nok-ree´)

RUTH 2:5–10

Her family traveled from Mexico—migrant workers my dad rescued from the borders of life and death. I'm fairly certain the "rescue" wasn't legal at the time. But paperwork would later be completed permitting their stay.

Her name was Adella. She was two years older than me, but we loved to play together despite our age difference and language difficulties. Actually, I don't recall we talked much, but somehow we had no problem communicating. Whenever I rode out with my dad to his hog farm, he would work, and Adella and I would play. We loved climbing into the giant, empty grain silos.

We'd turn a silo into a house. We swept the dirt floor and chased the mice. I'm sure I was filthy when I got home . . . nothing like dry, red, dusty Oklahoma farmland in need of rain.

My dad's farm didn't survive, and our family moved. Thirty years passed before I saw my childhood friend again. Her family never left the small town, and in later years she actually served as a caregiver for my grandfather.

We met again at his funeral. We embraced for a long time, and she told me how much she loved my grandfather. We had a new bond to share.

Years after the funeral, while we were sitting around the table during Christmas dinner, my dad told us with tears in his eye how Adella had thanked him for saving her family. My dad and I haven't always seen eye to eye, and he hasn't always done the right thing, but this time he did.

My friend, Adella, was a *nokriy*, an alien in a foreign land whose family had come to stay. I'm so glad they did.

Digging for treasure

1. Read Ruth 2:5–7. What was Boaz's first question after he greeted his harvesters?

Don't you love it? She caught his eye right away. Maybe he noticed her because of where she gleaned.

2. According to the foreman, where did Ruth ask to glean?

3. Read Ruth 2:2. Where did Ruth plan to glean?

4. Read Leviticus 19:9. What was the law? What was left for the poor and aliens?

Yet, Ruth planned and asked to glean "among the ears of grain" and "among the sheaves behind the harvesters." Jewish commentators explain that her request to the foreman exceeded biblical law. They maintain, "Some interpreters suggest that her request was a ploy to meet the owner of the field, since special permission to glean among the sheaves is granted in 2:15."[1]

What do you think? Is Ruth more cunning than we thought? Or do you think she's oblivious to the weight of her requests?

Regardless of her motives, we do know she asked. Nothing is wrong with asking, right? I tell my kids this all the time. The answer we receive may be a "no," but you'll never know if you don't ask.

I really like Ruth's spunk. I wonder how much of her desperation for food and better living conditions and her love for Naomi intensified her resolve. What are you like when you're hungry? Can you imagine the desperation when finding food for hungry loved ones?

5. According to the foreman, how long has Ruth worked in the field? Did she take a lot of breaks?

6. How does Boaz address Ruth (Ruth 2:8)? What does this term tell you?

Remember, she was not from *around these parts.* Even though Boaz knew she was a foreigner, he didn't speak of her as one. There was kindness in his voice.

7. What does he tell Ruth in verses 8 and 9?

"Don't go to another field. Stay here and follow my servants; they won't hurt you. Oh, and get a drink when you need one." His were words of acceptance. Safety. Provision.

8. Our answers will be purely speculation, but what do you think prompted Boaz's *chêsêd*?

9. What was Ruth's physical and spoken response (v. 10)?

Ruth called herself a foreigner (**5237**).

10. Locate the Hebrew word for **5237** in the Old Testament Dictionary in the back of this book. To whom did this term refer? How were these people regarded? What "emphasis" was placed with this word?

This word held negative connotations to say the least. It also quite simply denoted, "a permanent resident alien who had once been a citizen of another land."[2]

11. What does Ruth's response tell you about her?

We could learn so many lessons from this girl. She knew who she was, but that didn't stop her from accepting the gifts granted her. She wasn't looking back toward Moab. She seemed determined to live in Bethlehem. *Nokriy* implied she planned to stay, and her face planted on the ground demonstrated her humility.

I prayed for years for my children to have humble confidence. Nobody likes people who are brash and rude in their self-assurance, but the other end of the scale, fear due to a lack of assurance, can be just as off-putting—especially if that person oozes talent. I've noticed this while watching music competitions on television. A contestant may have an amazing voice, but his or her lack of confidence weakens the performance and limits the audience's votes. But the opposite happens also. Those contestants whose confidence is over-the-top seem less appealing. America never chooses those people. I've noticed America votes for the ones with humble confidence.

Humble confidence pleases God, too.

Ruth seemed to have humble confidence—strong, unwavering. Yet, thinking back on today's lesson I'm struck with the thought that Boaz's kindness and acceptance humbled her. She knew her place; she knew she didn't belong, but his kindness set her on her knees, face to the ground.

Has anyone's kindness humbled you as Boaz's did Ruth? Explain.

Connecting with other Scripture

12. What does Titus 3:1–2 demand?

13. Read Titus 3:3–7. What changed the way the people lived?

Don't you love these words? "When the goodness[5544] and loving kindness[5363] of God our Savior appeared, he saved us . . ."

14. Locate **5544** in the New Testament Dictionary in the back of this book. Read the entire definition and summarize the meaning of this wonderful word describing our God.

" . . . It is the grace which pervades the whole nature, mellowing all which would have been harsh and austere."

Please take a deep breath and let it out slowly.

15. What does this word tell us about the nature of Christ and thus God?

16. Read Titus 3:4–7. What happened when God's kindness and love appeared?

17. Why did he save us?

18. Can you guess the Hebrew word tied with the Greek word that was translated "mercy" in verse 5? (Look back to Day 4.)

19. How did he save us?

20. How do we become heirs?

If we are heirs, then we are daughters.

What did Boaz call Ruth?

Yes, he called this *nokriy* a daughter. She was accepted.

What did he promise her?

He promised her safety and provision. But don't forget that his kindness was prompted by her actions. Ruth simply asked if she could glean in the fields—she petitioned for more than the normal provision. What would've happened if she had not asked and simply gleaned at the edge of the field? Would she have been noticed?

How many of us don't receive all that God has for us because we do not ask?

Ruth was not worthy. She was a foreigner. We are not worthy; we, too, are foreigners.

But . . .

21. Read Matthew 7:7–11. What is the promise in verse 8?

22. What kind of gifts will God give us?

Bringing the treasure home to our hearts

Years ago I discovered a wonderful practice in prayer. Life was a little difficult. I desperately needed the Lord's presence and provision, so I began every day on my knees. I didn't stay there long—just long enough to humble myself before him, to praise him, to ask forgiveness, and to petition for what was on my heart. It's been a wonderful habit. I know it's changed me.

A few months ago I held a 30-Day Knee Challenge on my blog. The challenge was to fall on our knees every morning before we did anything else. My husband took me up on the challenge, and he hasn't stopped. I've been humbled watching my humble man get on his knees, too. I'm on one side of the bed, he the other. But the sweetest thing about it is that even though he was a really good man before, I see him melting before God. His heart is changing. His spiritual ears are opening.

Can you think of a time when you humbled yourself before God, not out of fear, but because of his kindness? What happened?

If you want to experience the blessing of humbling yourself before the Lord, try the 30-Day Knee Challenge.

Let's pray together

"Dear God, thank you for noticing us. Thank you for calling us your daughters and welcoming us into your harvest even though we are each a *nokriy* (nok-ree´)—we don't belong. May we have humble confidence as we come to you in prayer. We know your nature is kind, good, loving, sacrificial, and providing. Lead us today. Forgive us our insecurities. We are secure in you. Amen."

To Trust

Châsâh (kaw-saw´)

RUTH 2:11–12

Even the best marriages require elbow grease.

It seems God enjoys placing polar opposites together for life, as if being man and woman were not enough. I'm convinced that love blinds us to our differences until we've proclaimed our vows and moved into the same house. I'm also persuaded that couples divorce after decades of marriage because they "put up" with their spouse's quirks hoping for a change that never came. So after thirty years, when the children are grown, they divorce.

My husband and I couldn't be farther apart on the personality scale. I knew it was bad, but I didn't know how bad until we took personality tests during a ministerial preparation weekend. As we entered the counseling room to discuss our personalities, the two counselors' expressions were grave. We were seated, and one psychologist reached out to touch my hand. With all sincerity he looked into my eyes and asked, "How are you doing? Are you okay?"

I burst into laughter. (Probably not the correct response.) It was the most freeing and wonderful moment. I responded, "I'm okay now, but you should've asked me fifteen years ago!"

My Mike is very intelligent. He's Chinese. And he was in the military. Those attributes summarize him well. He's a numbers man, but he can also spell and pronounce words like a dictionary, and he's always correcting me. I'm a touchy-feely, go-with-the-flow, sensitive type, and his corrections used to offend me. Actually, my pride took the offense until I realized that this was not a competition.

One day the epiphany of all epiphanies cleared up my husband's "pickiness" offenses against me when I realized he corrects me because he loves me. He wants me to succeed as a writer and speaker. He's not in competition with me (though I am with him at times). He does what he does because he loves me.

I had to choose to believe this, and there are still days when I must choose to believe that his intentions are good, though those days have become fewer and farther between. I have to trust, *châsâh,* that he loves me.

By God's grace, despite both of our quirks, we've been married almost a quarter of a century. I truly believe that my *châsâh* in God led me to trust my husband's love. He opened my eyes to Mike's loving ways, once offensive, because I desperately trusted God himself.

Digging for Treasure

1. Read Ruth 2:10–11. What reasons did Boaz give for his kindness to Ruth?

2. What do we know about Boaz's character (his background and the way he greeted his servants) that makes his favor toward Ruth likely?

3. Read Ruth 2:12. What does Boaz hope for Ruth?

4. What does Ruth's move to Bethlehem prove to Boaz?

"The Lord repay you for what you have done, and a full reward be given you by the Lord, the God of Israel, under whose wings you have come to take refuge![2620]" (v. 12)

Don't you love this imagery? It's found throughout the Psalms.

5. Find **2620** in the Old Testament Dictionary in the back of this book and summarize the definition.

Most Bibles translate verse 12 as the *English Standard Version* has above. They use the English words "take refuge." The imagery is beautiful and connotations powerful, but how does a person take refuge under the wings of an invisible God?

Another definition of *châsâh* and the *King James Version* gives a tangible answer to this ethereal expression.

châsâh: "to flee (for protection), seek refuge, to trust in, confide in, hope in (someone). Mostly used in the spiritual sense of seeking spiritual refuge and putting trust in God."[1]

"The Lord recompense thy work, and full reward be given thee of the Lord God of Israel, under whose wings thou art come to trust." (Ruth 2:12 KJV)

6. According to the *King James Version* and this definition, how do we take refuge under God's wings?

I love the imagery of seeking refuge under God's wings, but the beautiful picture meets reality with the definition "putting trust in God." Placing oneself under God's wings really means *trusting* him.

7. Why do you think Ruth put her trust in Naomi's God?

8. Is God blessing Ruth for that trust? How?

Can you think of a time in your life when God blessed you for trusting him? Explain.

Has there been a time when you didn't trust God but wish you had?

9. Does the imagery of "taking refuge" under God's wings help you trust him? Please describe your thoughts.

Connecting with other Scripture

Read Psalm 91:1–4 to answer the following questions.

10. What will those who "dwell in the shelter" of God do? (v. 1)

11. Why can the psalmist call God "my refuge and my fortress? (v. 2)

12. From what will God save him? (v. 3)

"For he will deliver you from the snare[6341] of the fowler and from the deadly pestilence[1698]" (v. 3).

13. Look up **6341** in the Old Testament Dictionary in the back of this book. What does this Hebrew word mean literally and figuratively?

". . . net, snare, trap; anything which causes someone to fall."[2]

14. Locate **1698** in the Old Testament Dictionary. How did the prophets frequently use this word?

15. Now that we know the meaning of the ancient words, what does trusting in God save us from? Why?

16. Where does the psalmist find refuge or trust? (v. 4)

17. How do you crawl up under God's wings?

18. What will be the psalmist's shield and rampart? (NIV)

19. How can God's faithfulness be a shield and buckler? (KJV)

Can you think of a time when trusting in God's faithfulness protected you? What's your testimony?

Ruth doesn't have much personal history with the God of the Jews; it's probably not her personal testimony that grants her wisdom to trust God but rather the testimony of other believers. Can't you imagine that for at least ten years Naomi, and hopefully her sons, told stories of their faithful God to Ruth and Orpah? Perhaps as they lived *guwr* in Moab they continued to celebrate Passover and other Jewish holidays—all of which point to the faithfulness of God.

Assuredly other people's testimonies have inspired me to keep on keepin' on. But my faith has grown because of those desperate days when I made a choice. I could do things my way or God's way. I could be mad at him or trust he is always good. I could demand my way or wait. I could quit or keep on believing.

That's the hardest and most wonderful thing about trust. It's always our choice.

Bringing the treasure home to our hearts

List all the reasons you can trust God.

List all the reasons you aren't yet able to trust God.

Let's pray together

"*'Eloyhim* (el-o-heem), *Adonay* (ad-o-noy ´), *Shadday* (shad-dah ´ee), <u>God</u> who created us; <u>Lord</u> who desires relationship with us; <u>God</u> who is in control and all-powerful, forgive our distrust. We've not known peace because we've not climbed under your wings. How many times have we slipped from your protection because we only trusted ourselves? Lord, if for no other reason, we can *chasah* (kaw-saw ´) in you because you sent Jesus. We are saved for all eternity. Help us trust you so we may not fall or experience your judgment. Be our shield and buckler. Help us trust you as Ruth did. Amen."

Spoken with the Heart

Lêb (labe)

RUTH 2:13

She asked me to come because she had something important to tell me. I'd only been sitting on her couch for a few minutes when she whispered, "I'm going to divorce Keith." My heart fell to the pit of my stomach. I knew depression weighed her down; she wasn't happy. He was deployed for months at a time. He was never home, and we lived in a foreign country. It was lonely.

I really don't remember the rest of our conversation. I don't think I stayed long. Sometimes the right words won't come, and it's better to say nothing at all. But the rest of the day I walked around burdened. God wouldn't free me.

Honestly, I don't know to what extent religion or God swayed my feelings that day. Maybe my resolve was due to our close living conditions in our German townhomes. We spent almost every afternoon together. I'd come to know my friend's marriage better than most, and I could see the two sides of this story.

I ambled back across our yards and hesitantly knocked on her back door. It was nap time. No kids in sight. We sat down on her couch again next to the giant picture window that looked out on the backyard with its empty swingset.

Tears filled my eyes. My voice quivered as I told her, "God does not want you to divorce Keith."

Decades have passed since that painful day. Their marriage, still intact, has not been trouble-free. But miracles haven't ceased, and each day they both grow closer to God and to each other. Old wounds are healing.

I'm sure my words were not what convinced her to stay. My friend is not one easily persuaded. At other times, she's not taken my advice.

She told me my tears were what changed her mind. My tears revealed that my words were spoken with my *lêb*. She knew that my heart was fully involved.

Digging for treasure

1. Read Ruth 2:10–13. Do you think Ruth is still on her knees in verse 13? Why?

2. In what level of society does Ruth place herself as she talks to Boaz?

3. Do you think her humility affects Boaz? Does humility or lack thereof affect the way you treat someone?

I have a confession. Do you remember the story about the lady I worried was conning me—the story introducing *chêsêd*? Well, I've continued to help her through the years, but lately, I've not had the grace nor the time. Most of all, I think my heart has hardened because I don't feel she is humble. Isn't that weird? She's so needy, so poor. But her demands make it difficult to *want* to give. I know my relationship with her is a work in progress. Please pray for me to have a generous heart and wisdom. Pray for her, too. Her name is Eulandra.

I feel better already knowing that you are praying for her and me.

4. In verse 13, what does Ruth ask Boaz to do?

5. What does she say Boaz has given her?

6. How has he given her comfort?

7. How has he spoken to her?

There's that word: *kindly*. Let's find out what Hebrew word was translated here.

8. Locate **3820** in the Old Testament Dictionary in the back of this book. What does it mean?

This definition unpacks the word with greater detail:

> "*Lēḇ:* a shortened form of the word *lēḇāḇ*, 'heart.' The heart, the center, the middle of something. This word and its correlate, *lēḇāḇ*, signify the physical heart. *Lēḇ*, however, is more commonly used for the center of <u>man's inner or immaterial nature.</u> This usage has passed into common English with expressions such as 'heart and soul,' 'the heart goes out [to someone],' 'his heart is in the right place,' . . ."[1]

9. How would you translate this verse? What would you write instead of "kindly"?

10. What has Boaz done beyond what was required of him in the Law?

Do you know anybody like this? A person who gives generously from the heart beyond what is required?

Connecting with other Scripture

11. Read Luke 11:33–36. How do you interpret these verses? What do you think Jesus was teaching?

I hope by now you've discovered that reading different translations as well as looking into the definitions of the ancient words helps us understand meaning. Yet, though we may find the definitions of the Greek or Hebrew words, sometimes meaning is lost because Jesus taught through Jewish idioms or customs. Teacher and historian Ray Vander Laan opened my eyes to this truth in his teachings, *That the World May Know*. But another resource that has helped me dig through the mysteries of Jesus' teachings is the *Complete Jewish Bible*. Read how translator David H. Stern interprets these verses:

> "No one who has kindled a lamp hides it or places it under a bowl; rather, he puts it on a stand, so that those coming may see its light. The lamp of your body is the eye. When you have a 'good eye,' [that is, when you are generous,] your whole body is full of light; but when you have an 'evil eye,' [when you are stingy,] your whole body is full of darkness. So, take care that the light in you is not darkness! If, then, your whole body is

filled with light, with no part dark, it will be wholly lighted, as when a brightly lit lamp shines on you" (Luke 11:33–36 CJB).

12. According to the *Complete Jewish Bible*, what does it mean to have a good eye and an evil one?

13. Have you experienced the feelings of light and darkness when you were generous or stingy? Explain.

I was so excited when I read David Stern's translation of these verses. I could relate. I've literally experienced darkness in my stinginess and light and warmth when I've been generous. I much prefer the feeling generosity leaves. But I am human. My heart is human. My eyes, too.

What's the first word (or second) out of a toddler's mouth? If I remember correctly, my children learned how to say "no." And then without any instruction, they learned how to say, "Mine!" That was the first time I understood original sin. We are born with a stingy, selfish nature.

But Jesus.

But the Holy Spirit.

But God.

14. Read Ezekiel 11:19. What did God promise?

15. In Ezekiel 11:20 God says that with their new hearts, his people will "walk in my statutes and keep my rules and obey them." Read Matthew 7:12. According to Jesus, what sums up the Law?

16. Does Jesus' summation of the Law remind you of a Hebrew word we've studied?

17. Read Galatians 5:22–23. Name the fruits of the Spirit.

18. How do these fruits relate to *chêsêd?*

The presence of the Holy Spirit in us changes our hearts. Our hearts of stone are replaced by hearts of flesh . . . porous, soft, and shapeable. Good things—God things—come out of a heart changed by his Spirit. The book of Ruth is a true story about real people found in the lineage of Jesus, but it's also an allegory. Our dear Boaz represents Christ. If you ever need a picture of Jesus, envision Boaz and his goodness, kindness, strength, wealth, and honor. Perhaps picturing Boaz will also help us identify the Holy Spirit, who takes residence in us when we make Christ our Savior.

19. Describe Boaz's heart from what we've studied.

Bringing the treasure home to our hearts

Describe a time when you were generous. What motivated you? How did you feel afterward?

Do you find it easy to give or is it hard for you?

I've discovered that generosity is often a "learned" trait. Looking back to my parents and grandparents, I know I inherited a "careful" (I don't want to say "stingy") heart. But that "careful" heart has stopped my generous spirit at times.

Were you taught to be generous or careful?

Let's pray together

"Oh, Lord, thank you for the story of Ruth. Thank you for painting a picture of your kindness and generosity in the person of Boaz. We want to be like that, generous and kind-hearted. Forgive us when we don't give freely, when stinginess pervades our spirits, when our eyes are dark. Fill us with your Spirit of light. Replace our hardened hearts with generous ones not just for *our* pleasure, but for the blessing of others that they might see a glimpse of you in our actions. Let us demonstrate generosity for the generations to come. Let us give with a generous *lêb* (labe). Amen."

Oh, for Someone to Notice You

Nakar (naw-kar)

RUTH 2:14–19

My daughter's paintings take your breath away. Yes, I'm a proud momma, but I promise, I'm not just proud—it's true. But her gift wasn't discovered (I don't think she even knew what was inside her) until our family moved from Boston to North Carolina after Mike's retirement from the Army.

It was a difficult move for Lauren—October of her high school senior year. We hoped to make the move earlier, but God's calendar was not the same, and no job offer came. As the summer ended and it became clear we weren't moving before school started, I insisted Lauren finish the projects required for an AP Art class in Massachusetts. It was a small battle. But my daughter complied.

But months later when we moved to North Carolina and enrolled the kids in school, we learned that the new high school did not offer an accelerated Art class. We were disappointed, yet we enrolled her in another art class.

Weeks passed. Lauren trudged through life until one day she came home telling me about her new art teacher, Ms. Hewitt. Only two or three years out of college, she was pretty, talented, kind, and loved Jesus. "Ms. Hewitt wants to treat me as an AP Art student!" Lauren squealed.

This meant my daughter would create twenty-five special art projects in different media centered around a theme. Lauren chose to paint the people back home in Massachusetts on cardboard, which represented our moving boxes.

She had never painted faces before, but suddenly her room was filled with amazing portraits. I have no doubt Ms. Hewitt taught her techniques, but I also know we wouldn't have discovered this gift if this one teacher had not *nākar* my daughter. She took notice of her. She saw the possibilities, she supplied the special provision, and Lauren's life would never be the same.

Digging for treasure

1. Read Ruth 2:14. What kindness did Boaz extend to Ruth at the meal?

Can you imagine how hungry Ruth was when Boaz offered bread and roasted grain? It was the tastiest bread and grain she'd placed in her mouth! Have you ever experienced such hunger?

2. Read Ruth 2:15–16. What orders did Boaz give his men? Does any of the orders seem extreme?

3. Read Ruth 2:17–18. How long did Ruth work? What did she do after she gathered the barley?

4. How much grain did she carry home? What else did she bring Naomi?

According to my Bible's study notes, an *ephah* is about twenty-two liters. Can you imagine carrying eleven two-liter Coke bottles? I don't like carrying four! She was one strong lady. And prudent. Ruth didn't have to cook supper when she got home; she brought leftovers for Naomi. I dread cooking after a long, hard day's work.

A good friend of mine pointed out that because of Ruth, leftovers are biblical (in case your family refuses to eat them).

5. Read Ruth 2:19. What did Naomi ask Ruth?

6. How did Naomi know that the owner of the field "took notice" of Ruth?

Ruth came home to Naomi with her arms full. Her day was more than success-ful. It was obvious she'd been granted special privileges, beyond what was required; Naomi implied this. "Blessed be the man who <u>took notice</u> of you." Took notice" was employed to translate *nāḵar*. Read this definition:

> "*nāḵar:* to scrutinize, observe, examine, recognize; to disguise oneself. Basically denotes physical apprehension (recognition), whether through sight, touch, or hearing. *Nāḵar* can indicate a visual inspection <u>with the intention of recognizing something or someone</u> . . . also means to acknowledge."[1]

7. Knowing the definition, would you change the translation of verse 19? How would you write it?

I personally like "took notice." If I were to change it I would need more than two words to explain the word *nākar*. Boaz's notice of Ruth was more than visual. His notice affected his actions big time; he definitely acknowledged her sacrificial character.

"Take notice" sometimes implies more than the literal meaning, as English can also hold meaning beyond the words themselves.

Has anyone ever taken notice of you? Maybe a teacher, an employer, a neighbor? Please share your story.

I pray that as you work through this study you are beginning to experience the living God and his hand in your life. He's taken notice of you. The Bible is filled with story after story of people *nākar* by God. One particular story sits close to my heart. I love the tenderness, justice, and faithfulness God demonstrates when he meets Hagar in the desert.

Connecting with other Scripture

8. Read Genesis 16:3–13. Summarize this story in your own words.

9. What does the angel of the Lord ask Hagar in verse 7? Why does he ask her this?

Does God ever ask you questions when you are praying? God's questions bring clarity and set the stage for his response, his help.

10. What name does Hagar give God? Why?

This is so rich. I can hardly stand it. We have to do some digging.

"So she called the name of the LORD who spoke to her, 'You are the God[410] of seeing[7210] for she said, 'Truly here I have seen[7200] him who looks after[7200*] me" (Genesis 16:13).

* The *English Standard Version* edition of the *Key Word Study Bible* recognizes the Hebrew word in this verse as **7210**, but the *King James Version* edition with Strong's and the *New King James Version* edition, both identify **7200.**

11. Locate these three numbers in the Old Testament Dictionary in the back of this book. Write the Hebrew word and the applicable definitions.

410:

7210:

7200:

Rewrite Genesis 16:13, replacing the English counterparts with the corresponding Hebrew words.

12. What is the difference between *rŏi'y* and *râ'ah?* Why would Hagar use two different words?

I've always loved this Scripture passage because there's just something important about being seen, noticed. Nothing feels worse than feeling invisible. I'm sure Hagar felt invisible in Abram and Sarai's home. The harsh treatment she experienced made her feel even worse, until God took notice. But God did more than take notice. According to the definition of *râ'ah*, God did more than see Hagar. She felt God *understood* her and *provided for* her.

Connecting with other Scripture

13. Let's turn to the New Testament and experience a moment when Jesus saw and *understood* the pain of those around him. Read John 11:32–35. What happened when Jesus saw Mary and the others mourning?

14. Did it trouble Jesus to see his friends mourn, or was it something else?

There is no other religion in the world such as ours. We have a personal, identifiable, authentic God. He's a God who sees us. He takes notice—*nākar*. But his *nākar* is more than vision. God's *nākar* accompanies a heart that understands.

We've mentioned it before, but I believe Boaz took notice of, or favored, Ruth because his own mother was a foreigner. He admired Ruth, but maybe he also *understood* her—at least more than any other Jewish man in Bethlehem that day.

Bringing the treasure home to our hearts

How do you know that God has taken notice of you?

Write a prayer of thanksgiving to Jesus for seeing you and knowing you, or write a prayer asking that he show you that he notices you. He is faithful.

Let's pray together

"*El Rŏ'iy* (El-Ro-ee), the God who sees us, thank you. We're so thankful for your careful watch, that you *nāḵar* (naw-kar), but Lord, we are even more thankful for your understanding. You are our *El Râ'âh* (El-Raw-aw'). What God cares enough to understand his people? We thank you for Jesus. We love you. Strengthen our faith. Deepen our heart-knowledge of you. Amen."

Kindness to the Living and the Dead

Chêsêd (kheh´-sed)

RUTH 2:20

Have you received *chêsêd* and not wanted it? Confession. I have.

I know my situation is not unique. Divorces and blended families are an accepted part of our culture. But my parents divorced after thirty-six years of marriage. Needless to say, though I was all grown up, it stung. And when each parent remarried, it was weird.

I remember grieving those first few months. I'd see older couples walking hand in hand, and the fact that my parents weren't one of those couples anymore sat heavy on my heart. If during all those years of marriage there had ever been an elephant in the room ignored by all, I didn't see it. Their divorce came as a shock. It was a shock for my mother, too, though she knew they had marital problems.

The divorce broke my mother's heart, but two years after my dad told her he didn't love her anymore, she married a man she trusted.

His track record in marriage lacked longevity. His first wife left him when their children were very young, but she granted him full custody of the kids. He raised three children alone.

My mom loved him for this. And so she married him.

They were married two years before my mom received a diagnosis of early-onset Alzheimer's. At sixty her personality began to change. She couldn't remember things. She battled the disease for seven years until God's *chêsêd* took her home.

Despite the short duration of their marriage, my mom's husband has faithfully played the stepdad role, though when they married I felt I could never call him a stepdad. He's visited our family, sent cards and gifts for birthday and Christmas, and attended graduations.

His personality is different from our family's; it's awkward when we're together. During a visit I complained to God, "Lord, he has no obligation to stay connected with us. Why is he still around?"

And the Lord gently replied as clear as day, "Because he won't leave. That's why she married him." My stepdad is a man of *chêsêd* to the living and the dead.

Digging for treasure

1. Read Ruth 2:19–20. Whom did Naomi wish the Lord would bless?

2. Why?

3. Was Naomi speaking of Boaz or God when she said, "He has not stopped showing kindness . . ."?

It's rather hard to interpret. This is an instance when translation proved difficult not because of meaning but because of the order of the ancient words. When order causes confusion, I compare with other translations. If you don't have a plethora of Bibles at home, they can be found at your fingertips with Web sites such as Biblegateway.com. However, the translation I found most helpful in this case can't be found on the Internet. It is the *Complete Jewish Bible*. I purchased mine on Amazon. Read how this translation interprets the verse: "Na'omi said to her daughter-in-law, 'May he be blessed by *Adonai,* who has not stopped showing grace, neither to the living or the dead'" (Ruth 2:20a CJB).

4. According to the *Complete Jewish Bible*, who had not stopped showing his kindness, God or Boaz?

5. What did this knowledge do for Naomi? Did her countenance change?

Has there been a time in your life when God seemed absent until a glimmer of hope arrived? What brought you hope?

6. Back to Ruth. How had God demonstrated his grace or kindness to the living and the dead?

7. Can you guess the Hebrew word translated in the *New International Version* as "kindness" and the *Complete Jewish Bible* as "grace"?

There it is . . . *chêsêd.*

8. List some of the definitions for *chêsêd*. (Look back to Day 4.)

But *chêsêd* was more than kindness, mercy, love, and grace. *Chêsêd* involved commitment, faithfulness. It often presupposed a relationship, but when the relationship didn't exist, the person demonstrating *chêsêd* acted as if it did.

> ". . . It is closely tied to His covenant with His chosen people; in fact, the covenant may be thought of as the relationship from which the *chêsêd* flows. God's *chêsêd*, however, is not bound by the covenant itself, and though men may prove unfaithful to this relationship, God's *chêsêd* is everlasting."[1]

9. If *chêsêd* presupposed a relationship, if it is closely tied to God's covenant with his chosen people, if God's faithfulness does not rely on ours, what does *chêsêd* tell you about God?

Read Ruth 2:20 again.

The *New International Version* reads, ". . . He has not stopped showing his kindness to the living and the dead." "Stopped showing" was translated from the word *'āzab*. Read the definition of this Hebrew word:

· *'āzab*: "to forsake, abandon, leave behind, desert."[2]

10. Rewrite Ruth 2:20 according to your new understanding of *'āzab*. How would you translate that sentence?

11. How did Naomi know God hadn't abandoned her and forsaken *chêsêd*?

Yep. Boaz was more than a nice man. He was one of the kinsman-redeemers.

12. Read Leviticus 25:23–25. Naomi no longer owned land. How could she get it back?

I wonder why Naomi didn't seek out her kinsman-redeemers the first day she arrived in Bethlehem. Maybe she felt too downhearted, embarrassed, or mad at God. What do you think?

But God was proving his faithfulness as he always does. Let's step out of our own world into the bigger picture. It's important that we believe in the faithfulness of God in our lives, but it's paramount we understand what is happening with Israel, his chosen people.

Connecting with other Scripture

13. Read Deuteronomy 7:7–8. Why did the Lord choose his people?

14. According to Deuteronomy 7:9, how long will God be faithful to those who love him and keep his commands?

15. From what we've learned today about God's *chêsêd,* does God still love Israel? How do you know?

16. Read Romans 11:1–12. Did the Israelites' rejection of Christ surprise God? Why?

17. Why would God do this? Why would he give them a "spirit of stupor"?

18. Did God reject his people? How do we know? (v. 5)

19. Read Romans 11:28–31. How does Paul describe God's gifts and callings? What hope does this give you?

If I understand Romans 11 correctly, God wasn't surprised when the Jews rejected Jesus. He allowed his favorites to reject Christ so the Gentiles would have a chance to receive grace. But the disobedience of Israel affords them the opportunity for grace, too—grace they didn't need or experience under the Law.

When Elimelech and Naomi moved to Moab, it didn't take God by surprise. He wasn't shocked or hurt. Maybe as they sold the house and packed their bags God rubbed his hands together. He knew their move would save a lost Moabitess woman named Ruth whose Gentile blood would one day pump through the veins of God's Son born in a stable.

These themes run throughout the Bible:

> God lets those he loves go, and they come back.
> He loves his own, but he always welcomes those not part of his chosen.
> Jesus ate with the sinners.
> He touched the lepers.
> He spoke to the Samaritan woman.
> He desires all to be saved, and he has a plan for that salvation.

Bringing the treasure home to our hearts

Is there someone you love who needs salvation? Who is it? Write your prayer for that person using the knowledge of God's *chêsêd*.

Let's pray together

"Jesus, Holy Spirit, thank you for your faithful *chêsêd* (kheh´-sed). We know you never abandon us or your lovingkindness. You are holy. You still demand our trust. We can't come to you and dwell with you without it, but you are always waiting. Bring the prodigals home. Give us a flicker of hope that you are still involved. We love you. Amen."

More Than Good

Tôwb (tobe)

RUTH 2:21–23

I was going to be rich.

It was the summer between my freshman and sophomore years in college, and a job transfer had moved my parents to a new town where I knew nobody. I didn't want to spend my summer friendless, alone with my parents, plus I wanted to earn some money. My dad wasn't opposed to me making money.

The plan seemed flawless.

I arranged to live with my sister and work at the grain elevator where her husband worked. It was five hours from my parents' new home. I didn't have friends there either, but dollar signs shone in my eyes. Wheat harvest always promised long hours, a good income, and cute *wheaties*. Handsome guys driving wheat trucks weren't my incentive, yet they sweetened the deal. I always dreamed of marrying a farmer. The summer held endless potential.

But wheat dust and my lungs didn't get along. After three weeks I could barely breathe. Only a few weeks into harvest I couldn't catch my breath without a prolonged coughing attack. I visited my sister's doctor. He wrote a prescription for antibiotics and told me I'd be fine, but the coughing grew more severe, and my body ached.

A week later my parents drove down for a visit. After they assessed my condition, I returned home with them, disappointed and frustrated. I had only made $500. But I consoled myself that $500 wasn't bad for only three weeks of work (though double the pay would have bought double the shoes).

After returning home, my cough grew more serious, and one day my face turned gray. Mom rushed me to the emergency room where we learned that if you can't breathe, you don't have to wait in line for very long. The nurses swooshed me into a room, took my vitals, and placed a mask on my face.

After three breathing treatments the doctor ordered, "Unless your life depends on it, do not *ever* work at a grain elevator. It's not good for you."

It wasn't *tôwb* for me. That wheat dust made me one sick college girl. Marrying a soldier instead of a farmer was a *tôwb* thing—a good thing. I'm sure the doctor would agree.

Digging for treasure

1. Read Ruth 2:21. How long did Boaz tell Ruth to stay in his fields?

2. Read Ruth 2:22. How did Naomi respond to Boaz's request? What reason did she give for Ruth to comply?

3. According to Ruth 2:23, what two harvests did Ruth work in Boaz's fields, and with whom did she live?

I wonder how long Ruth worked in Boaz's fields. How long is a harvest season? She worked through two. In Oklahoma wheat harvest only lasts a few weeks—usually around a month, but if it rains, it takes longer.

According to the biblical calendar, the length of the harvests in Bethlehem was similar. We can measure their length because the harvests were designated by The Festivals of Israel.

> "The Offering of Firstfruits took place at the beginning of the barley harvest and signified Israel's gratitude to and dependence upon God (Leviticus 23:9–14). It occurred seven weeks before Pentecost, but there was also an offering of firstfruits associated with the Feast of Weeks or Pentecost, in celebration with the wheat harvest."[1]

4. According to this commentary, how many weeks were between the barley and wheat harvests?

We know Ruth worked in Boaz's fields for seven weeks. Actually, she worked longer than that because the wheat harvest started seven weeks after the barley harvest began. I'm just "guess-timating," but if the barley harvest took seven weeks, it's possible the wheat harvest did, too. That would be fourteen weeks altogether. They didn't own combines back then. They harvested with a sickle.

5. Testing your math skills. How many months did Ruth possibly work beside Boaz's servants?

I estimate Ruth hung out in Boaz's fields close to three months. Maybe it was less, but it's quite possible that for about three months (mid-March through early June) Ruth shared lunch with Boaz and his servants.

6. Read Ruth 2:22. How did Naomi respond?

"It is good[2896] . . ."

7. Locate **2896** in the Old Testament Dictionary in the back of this book and write down the meanings of this Hebrew word that apply to the context of this Scripture, the meaning Naomi inferred.

8. Do you think she had anything else on her mind besides Ruth's safety?

This situation was good. It was safe for Ruth. It was practical, wise, but it's so much more than that—Boaz was a kinsman-redeemer.

9. Can you think of any reason why Naomi didn't try to manipulate this situation sooner?

I'm impatient. I'd like to blame it on our culture, but it's probably my personality. I often leap before I look, but my husband is the opposite. He takes forever to make his move. He studies and ponders before making a decision.

Despite my impatient nature, I appreciate Naomi's patience. I know; it doesn't last long—the next verse proves that. But she didn't start scheming right away. She took a moment to be thankful first.

These are the first Scripture passages in Naomi's story that reveal a thankful spirit. The bitterness began to wane. Her concern shifted from herself to Ruth; her eyes suddenly focused on someone else's needs. Love changes things. Surely she was appreciating this daughter-in-law more and more. Surely she was appreciating God.

A thankful spirit can be life-changing . . . miraculous!

> "Gratitude unlocks the fullness of life. It turns what we have into enough, and more. It turns denial into acceptance, chaos to order, confusion to clarity. It can turn a meal into a feast, a house into a home, a stranger into a friend. Gratitude makes sense of our past, brings peace for today, and creates a vision for tomorrow." ~Melody Beattie, author of *Codependent No More.*

Connecting with other Scripture

10. Read Psalm 107:1. Why should we give thanks to the Lord?

11. From today's study, what is the Hebrew word for "good"?

The definition is lengthy in the Old Testament Dictionary in the back of this book, but I would like to point out a few meanings: "joyful, lovely, merry, more, pleasant, precious, profitable, promise . . ."

Another dictionary gives these definitions: "pleasant, beautiful, excellent, lovely, delightful, joyful, fruitful, precious, cheerful, kind, correct, righteous; that which is good, right; virtue; happiness, pleasantness . . . wisdom."[2]

I love it. If I plug these definitions into Psalm 107:1, God is . . .

Pleasant,
Beautiful,
Excellent,
Lovely,
Delightful,
Joyful,
Kind,

Righteous,
That which is good . . .
Wisdom.

God's goodness is all these things. What stirs in your spirit?

Read Psalm 107:1 again.

12. What endures forever?

13. We have also studied this Hebrew word. Can you deduce from our studies the ancient word that's been translated as "love"?

Yep. *Chêsêd.*

14. Can you recall some of the definitions for *chêsêd* without looking back?

Forever is a long time. We are called to give thanks to God because his *chêsêd* never ends. Even when we can't feel it or see it, we give thanks. That's called *faith.*

15. Read 1 Thessalonians 5:16. What does Paul tell the Thessalonians to do?

16. Why does he tell them to be thankful?

17. Why would God desire for us to be thankful?

I can't resist. Read this verse from the *Complete Jewish Bible*: "Always be joyful. Pray regularly. In everything give thanks, for this is what God wants from you who are united with the Messiah Yeshua." (1 Thessalonians 5:16)

Have you experienced company or children who were not thankful for your sacrifice? How did it make you feel? Did you want them to come back?

God is certainly beyond our human feelings. But we are made in his image. It must be frustrating to him when we do not recognize our blessings—especially when we've received salvation by faith in Jesus. Yet I believe he desires thanksgiving from us not for his sake but for our own. He knows how it can change our perspective and our hearts.

I need to share the rest of the letter to the Thessalonians to you as translated in the *Complete Jewish Bible*. It seems a fitting way to end this lesson: "May the God of *shalom* (peace) make you completely holy—may your entire spirit, soul, and body be kept blameless for the coming of our Lord Yeshua the Messiah. The one calling you is faithful, and he will do it." (1 Thessalonians 5:23–24 CJB, addition mine)

He is faithful. Keep in mind that God waited patiently for Naomi to come around. He didn't leave her. He didn't punish her. He waited until her heart found thanksgiving again.

Bringing the treasure home to our hearts

Do you have a hard time thanking God for all your circumstances? Explain.

Write a prayer of thanksgiving to God even if it is difficult.

How do you feel after thanking him?

Let's pray together

"Lord, you are more than *tôwb* (tobe) and your *chêsêd* (kheh´-sed) will never end. Thank you for demonstrating your goodness and kindness, mercy and love. Thank you for the story of Ruth. Help us express thanksgiving every day no matter what the circumstances, and help us be thankful for the blessings of today before we try to manipulate tomorrow. Amen."

A Plan for Rest

Mānôah (maw-noʹ-akh)
RUTH 3:1

N obody tells you how hard it is to be a mom. Nobody.

I think there are two reasons for this:

- Some women find motherhood the most wonderful thing in the world; their newborns sleep through the night. They enjoy staying home all day with their little ones. It fits their personality. These women make the rest of us feel guilty for struggling with our blessing. So, we keep our mouths shut. We don't tell anyone that motherhood requires losing yourself (and your mind).

or

- Once we've survived those very difficult years, the memories of the traumatic days fade. Easier years trump the hard ones, and we simply forget how bad it really was.

However, I remember one day as if it were yesterday. My children were two and four, the third child not even a twinkle in my eye. My second slept better through the night than my first, and I no longer needed to pray for at least four hours of straight sleep. One morning as we enjoyed Sesame Street together a thought danced through my mind: "I can be a good mommy! I've just been tired all this time!"

That blessed moment strengthened me. That day I realized how much I needed a resting place, a *mānôah,* to fulfill the duties of this job called "Momma."

But honestly, even with six hours of sleep at night, I desperately needed a deeper rest in my spirit to raise my children. That *mānôah* was only found when I took time for Bible study, quiet time, or meditation (whatever you want to call it). I had to have it every day no matter how much sleep I got the night before.

I evolved into the nap Nazi, desperate for my quiet afternoon with only the sound of sleeping babies. Candle lit, Bible open, and coffee poured. Here I found my strength to carry on. During those afternoons I found a spiritual *mānôah* that energized me for the rest of the day . . . actually, for the rest of my life.

Digging for treasure

1. Read Ruth 3:1. In your own words, write what Naomi told Ruth.

2. Can you hear the change in Naomi's voice? Was this statement to Ruth spoken with a heavy heart or an excited one? How do you know? (What would she have said if it were drudgery?)

3. Read Ruth 1:8–9. What does Naomi wish for both Ruth and Orpah?

4. Do you think she feels obligated to help Ruth?

I do, but despite the obligation, Naomi sounds excited in my ears. I think you can probably hear it, too. I believe there are several reasons for her change of heart, but first, I want to show you a treasure.

Ruth 1:9 and 3:1 both contain the same Hebrew word, though translated differently in many translations.

- "The Lord grant that you may find <u>rest,</u> each of you in the house of her husband!" (Ruth 1:9 ESV)

- "My daughter, should I not seek <u>rest</u> for you, that it may be well with you?" (Ruth 3:1 ESV)

- "My daughter, should I not try to find a <u>home</u> for you, where you will be well provided for?" (Ruth 3:1 NIV)

"Home" and "rest" have been translated from the Hebrew word *mānôah,* which means "resting place" (CWSDOT).

5. Where does Naomi believe Ruth will find rest? Is this a better *resting place* than Naomi's original attempt in chapter 1? How?

Hold the resting place imagery. We must do some extra digging. I've found more treasure today. Maybe I'm being nit-picky, but what I've found speaks to my soul. I'm not sure why. Maybe I understand Naomi's feeling of responsibility.

6. According to your translation, why does Naomi want to find rest for Ruth? (Ruth 3:1)

> The NIV reads, ". . . where you will be <u>well provided for?</u>"
> The CJB reads, ". . . so that things will go well with you."
> The KJV reads, ". . . that it may be well with thee?"

All three translations explain Naomi's desire for a resting place for Ruth as desiring a secure life for her daughter-in-law. Her desire is not passive, however. It is active. We need to learn a little bit more about Hebrew to glean this insight.

Hebrew verbs take on different meaning according to the word's *stem*. Seven stems affect whether a word is active or passive. Don't worry; we aren't going to discuss all the stems, only two—the Qal and Hiphil stems. My purpose is to demonstrate the life and beauty of the ancient language and show how through translation and tradition, we've lost intended meanings.The Hiphil Stem expresses a <u>causative type of action</u> with an active voice while the Qal Stem is employed for simple action. For example:

> Qal Stem: He killed.
> Hiphil Stem: He caused death.

(A great website to help further understand Hebrew is: http://www.hebrew4christians.com)

The Hebrew word translated in Ruth 3:1 as "well provided for" or "so that things will go well with you," is one word: *yāṭab*. Here are its stems and uses:

1. to be good, be pleasing, be well, be glad

    (Qal)
    to be glad, be joyful
    to be well placed
    to be well for, be well with, go well with
    to be pleasing, be pleasing to
    (Hiphil)
    to make glad, rejoice
    to do good to, deal well with
    to do well, do thoroughly
    to make a thing good or right or beautiful
    to do well, do right[1]

Circle the fourth and fifth definitions of the Hiphil stem.

Remember Naomi's reasoning for Ruth and Orpah to return to Moab? She wanted them to find rest in another husband's home. Naomi feels responsible for Ruth. Granted, this is the first time she appeared worried about this girl since their return to Bethlehem, but none the less, her eyes have turned from her problems to Ruth's.

7. What happens with this verse when we plug in the Hiphil stem's fourth definition?

How would you translate this Hebrew word into English in Ruth 3:1?

If I translated this verse, I would've written, "My daughter, should I not find a home for you, to make things right." In other words, I believe Naomi said, "I owe you this. You've done so much for me. Let me try to make this good." I think this fits the context of the sentence as Naomi says, "Should I not try . . ." Her words reveal feelings of responsibility.

8. Whether or not the "Lee translation" holds merit, what is Naomi extending to Ruth? (It's a very important Hebrew word.)

Though no formal agreement (besides a marriage certificate) fueled this *chêsêd*, Naomi started to return Ruth's kindness. *Chêsêd* is like that. Naomi desired to find rest for her hard-working daughter-in-law. Rest that would last a lifetime.

Connecting with other Scripture

9. Read Hebrews 4:9–10. What remains for the people of God?

10. How does a person find such rest?

11. Read Hebrews 4:2–3. How do we enter God's rest?

12. What did Paul mean by "the Sabbath-rest"?

Paul wasn't referring to Saturday or Sunday or taking a day out of the week to rest. He was teaching about salvation. I remember the first time this Bible passage became clear to me. I wrote about it in my blog August 19, 2011:

> "There is nothing we can do to earn God's love and salvation. He wants us to *rest* in His love. He doesn't love Billy Graham any more than he loves a dying orphan in Africa or a convicted murderer who has given his life to Jesus.
>
> We cannot earn His love. We cannot read our Bibles enough, pray more, fast more often, heal people, preach and teach, share and care enough. Nothing makes God love us more or less. His love never changes. His love never wavers or ebbs and flows. Our ability to *feel* it may ebb and flow. But his love is constant. His grace is always there.
>
> The Law was set up to earn God's love. But Jesus came. And his Law *is* Love. His Law was: *rest* in the Love of God."

We are to simply rest in the love God gave through Jesus, our Kinsman-Redeemer. Jesus did the work. He is our *mānôah*—our resting place.

Do you find yourself trying to earn God's favor? What are some things you try to do?

13. Read James 2:14–26. Summarize this passage in your own words.

14. Why is "faith without works" dead?

We can't do anything to earn our salvation, but a believer benefits from pouring out God's love to others by helping those around her. God's *chêsêd* will naturally pour out of us. I believe this is what is happening to Naomi in chapter 3. She came home, back to her faith. It took a few weeks—maybe months—but her eyes were no longer focused on her losses. She's turned her focus inside out. This new perspective gave Naomi purpose, and life is better lived that way. Her circumstances have not changed yet, but hope is in the air, and joy is being restored to Mara. Purpose sweetens the bitter. It takes the edge off our pain.

Share a time when helping someone in need changed your focus and gladdened your heart.

Bringing the treasure home to our hearts

We've discovered two treasures today. What were they?

Which treasure do you struggle with the most, resting in God's salvation or focusing on your problems more than needs of those around you? Why?

Let's pray together

"God who sees us, who knows our hearts, we petition for your *mānôah* (maw-no'-akh) today. For those of us still striving to be good enough please take away the strife. Bring clarity in what Jesus did for us on the cross. We can't earn your love or salvation. Help us accept it. Turn our focus inside out, and give us your grace to help others find their home in you, their *mānôah* (maw-no'-akh). Amen."

A Ninja Plan

Yāda' (yaw-dah´)

RUTH 3:2–3

I wish I were Jewish. I think the Jewish people have wisdom about themselves unlike any people on Earth. One of my favorite books is written by a rabbi. The book is called *Yearnings: Embracing the Sacred Messiness of Life,* written by Rabbi Irwin Kula.

With sage-like wisdom Kula does what rabbis (rabbanim) do best. He places more questions in your mind than answers. Jesus did this when he taught, too. The next time you read a gospel, watch how he answers (or doesn't answer) many of the Pharisees' questions.

On my coffee table are books ranging from devotionals to Bible studies to nonfiction inspirational books to fiction. I've fallen in love with the library.

During my quiet time I ask the Lord which one he wants me to read, and I find golden nuggets in the pages he leads me to. The other morning I picked up *Yearnings,* and this is the paragraph I read:

> "In the Jewish tradition there are hundreds of names (for God): Father,
> Mother, Lover, Creator, Destroyer, Nurturer, Redeemer, Forgiver, Friend,
> Life-Giver, to name just a few. The name used most often in Jewish texts
> is also the most mysterious and intimate. It is YHWH, which in English

is all consonants and no vowels. In Hebrew it's actually a word with no consonants and all vowels. Either way, it is unpronounceable. When you try to say it, you hear the sound of breath, a simple exhale. What is this teaching? The name of God is not meant to be uttered. YWHW is not meant to be known. YHWH is meant to be breathed."[1]

You might want to argue that God does want to be known. That is his desire. But the point Kula makes isn't whether God wants us to know him, but that even with all our study and searching, he will never be fully understood this side of eternity. Yet he desires to be more than known; he desires to fill us as air fills our lungs.

I love theology, but Rabbi Kula released me from any presupposed ideas that I could ever grasp it all. So I've decided that when life starts tumbling out of control, and I began wondering what God is doing, I'm going to close my eyes and breathe.

Inhale. Exhale. Inhale deeper. Exhale longer.

And I will ask the Holy Spirit to let me smell God, breathe Jesus, be filled by the Holy Spirit. Because on this side of eternity, God cannot be fully *yâda*. He's not hiding in the shadows—he's simply more than our finite brains can handle. Hallelujah!

Digging for treasure

1. Read Ruth 3:2–3. What does Naomi tell Ruth to do?

2. Do you think Naomi is jumping the gun—trying to force Boaz's hand? Do you think her plan is wrong, or do you see wisdom in her scheme?

3. Why shouldn't Ruth wait for Boaz to possibly propose? Are there any indications about his character that makes this plan safe and necessary?

We don't know Boaz's age. One Jewish *midrash,* a rabbinical interpretation filling in the gaps of a biblical story, theorized that Boaz was in his eighties and Ruth in her forties. I can't quite picture Boaz that old, but we do know he was an older man who never married. Does it make you wonder why he never married? He's a good man, wealthy, well-liked, but single. Why?

I propose that Naomi discerned Boaz's character. She knew he would never propose to Ruth—he never was the marrying type. (Though some commentators theorize he was married, we're sticking to the black and white text here. No wife was mentioned.) Naomi also knew he was a good man. He wouldn't take advantage of Ruth. Boaz was a gentleman.

4. Read Ruth 3:3. When could Ruth reveal herself to Boaz according to Naomi's instruction?

Naomi planned for Boaz to be fully satisfied, perhaps a little tipsy, and sleepy when Ruth stepped out of the shadows. She smelled good. Clean. Dressed pretty. Her appearance would reveal her purpose. She wore no work clothes that night. Ruth dressed for a date even though Boaz was clueless.

As much as I hate to do this, so much mystery hangs around this story that I must reveal something I found digging into the ancient text. Before I do so, just let me say, I will give reasons why I don't believe Ruth and Boaz consummated a marriage. But there are so many sexual connotations; I believe that is what Naomi intended.

Notice the difference in translations:
> ". . . Then go down to the threshing floor, but <u>don't let him know you are there</u> until he has finished eating and drinking." (Ruth 3:3 NIV)
> ". . . and go down to the threshing floor, but <u>do not make yourself known</u>[3045] to the man until he has finished eating and drinking." (Ruth 3:3 ESV)

5. What's the difference between these translations?

Our own biases color the way we read our Bible, and commentators and translators are no different. I don't think any of us wants to believe something happened here at the threshing floor, but look at the definitions of the Hebrew word translated as "know" and tell me what you see. Also, keep in mind the ESV translation—*to be known*.

6. Look up **3045** in the Old Testament Dictionary in the back of this book.

- How many times is this word used in the Bible?

- What is its simple meaning?

- What is one of its primary uses?

- How can this word refer to knowing another person?

"*Yada*ʿ: to perceive, understand, know, discern, be known . . . to know sexually (i.e., have intercourse with). One of the most important Hebrew roots in the OT, *yâdaʿ* expresses a variety of meanings about various types of knowledge, including God's knowledge of man . . ."[2]

7. What do you think? Did Naomi instruct Ruth to be sneaky like a ninja, "Don't let him see you," or was she saying, "Don't let him <u>know you intimately</u> until he's had some wine"?

Desperate times call for desperate measures? I don't know. I would have to be beyond desperate to do what these words imply. But Ruth was one step ahead of Naomi. We'll have to wait a day to uncover Ruth's wisdom, but until then, let's discover how God knows us and desires we know him.

Connecting with other Scripture

8. Read 1 Corinthians 13:12. How does Paul describe our vision now?

9. How does he describe our knowledge?

10. How does he describe God's knowledge of us?

11. When will we know fully?

12. Read 1 Corinthians 8:1–3. What man is known by God?

13. Read Jeremiah 1:4–5. When did God know Jeremiah?

14. Read Psalm 139. How does God know you? Write down your favorite verses.

I love the thought of being known by God. But I also look forward to that day when we will stand face to face, and I will know him fully as he knows me now. The thought drifts beyond my comprehension.

Bringing the treasure home to our hearts

In today's lesson, Naomi formed a plan to force Boaz's hand. Are there times in our lives when it's okay to stop waiting on God and step out in faith? Give either a biblical or personal example that worked or backfired.

Honestly, I know there are days when I must wait on God; he can make everything fall into place. But I also know he gives opportunities that require my effort. Many of us believe that if we need to work for the dream, it's not from God. We hold this misconception that everything should fall into place easily. But the truth is, sometimes God cracks a door open, yet requires us to push in order to cross the threshold. Naomi and Ruth spotted the crack, and they pushed.

Has God cracked any doors for you lately, but you're waiting for them to magically fly open? Does this lesson free you to use your muscles?

Let's pray together

"Search us, O God, and *yâda*ʿ (yaw-dah´) our hearts! Try us and know our [anxious] thoughts. And see if there be any grievous way in us, and lead us in the way everlasting! Amen." (Psalm 139:23–24, plural pronouns mine).

"P.S. And Lord, please shut all doors not in your plan, but grant us the courage to push open the door you've cracked."

The Uncovering

Gâlâh (gaw-law)
RUTH 3:4

Does a childhood memory haunt you? When you attempt to replay it, do the details disappear—it's fuzzy, but your emotions have survived the years? My memory isn't the scary kind of haunting but the embarrassing sort. Even though I'm an adult and have raised three children, and I know how carefree children can be, especially gregarious ones such as I was—it's still a strange memory.

I think I was five. As I faintly recall, my mom and I were the only ones home on a late Saturday afternoon. Our family must have had plans for that night because Mom was taking a bath. I was hanging out with her waiting my turn. My clothes were off. I was *gâlâh*.

Suddenly, the doorbell rang. For a moment we froze. Silence. We waited. The doorbell rang again. Then I did it. I don't remember if my mom tried to stop me, but rather than ignoring the visitor, I gallivanted out of the bathroom . . . in my birthday suit.

Our pastor, a very good friend of the family, my best friend's dad, stood at the back door—the sliding glass door was open with only the screen closed, so we could talk even though he was not inside the house. I can't remember a thing we said.

But I do remember justifying my nakedness: *I'm only a little kid. It's okay that I'm standing here naked in front of Pastor Jerry.* But something else inside me knew I really should be covered with a towel at least. Despite these thoughts there I stood.

Though at first I positioned behind a recliner, I got so bold as to come out from behind the chair and continue chatting. Completely *gâlâh*.

He didn't come in. He didn't stay long. Perhaps he realized that it wasn't a good time.

And I realized that I'd crossed an invisible line—some sort of rite of passage. I learned that I had grown past the point of parading in front of adults in my birthday suit. Next time I'd grab a towel or just act as if no one were home. I couldn't run around *gâlâh* any more.

Digging for Treasure

1. Read Ruth 3:4. What does Naomi tell Ruth to do?

2. Does any of this seem strange to you?

3. If you were Ruth, would you have done what Naomi told you? Why or why not?

4. Why do you think Ruth agreed with this plan?

Naomi and Ruth had suffered much together. They had shared a home for years agonizing through infertility, no children/grandchildren, death, grief, and widowhood. They had traveled together! You learn a lot about a person when you travel with them—especially long, dusty trips like theirs. There is no doubt that at this point they trusted each other.

Do you have someone like this in your life? Who?

Let's see what the Law said about a woman proposing to her kinsman-redeemer.

5. According to Deuteronomy 25:5–10, what were the duties of the brother-in-law?

6. What name would be given to the first son she bore from that marriage? Why?

7. What could the woman do if her brother-in-law refused?

8. What would the woman do if the brother-in-law refused the elders at the city gate?

9. What name would be given to the family?

Can you picture it? She can take off one of his sandals and . . . spit in his face!

It seems ridiculous to us. But do we have any cultural humiliation like this?

My reason for our reading the Deuteronomy passage was not to give us a giggle, but to point out the fact that it wasn't uncommon for women to force the issue. It was legal for the woman to ask and even demand marriage. This passage will help us understand Boaz's actions later. He was a man who followed the Law to the letter.

10. Read Ruth 3:4 once more. According to your translation, what part of Boaz's body was Ruth told to uncover?

This whole scene sets us on the edge of our seats. Wait until you read all the meanings and connotations of the word translated as "uncover." I warn you. This is not a G-rated movie. ". . . Then go and uncover[1540] his feet and lie down, and he will tell you what to do." (Ruth 3:4b)

11. Look up **1540** in the Old Testament Dictionary in the back of this book. How is this term used "on occasion"?

Anyone blushing yet? Want to know more? If not, turn to the next page.

Again, let me state: I do not believe Ruth and Boaz consummated a marriage on this night, but it indeed seemed to be Naomi's intentions. Maybe she was aware of the other kinsman higher in the line, and she wanted to make sure that Boaz would be the one Ruth married. We will never know this side of heaven what was the actual intent or events, but respectable resources explain the tradition and possibilities.

The *NET Bible* is a wonderful resource that explains translators' reasons for word choices. It's found online and easy to use. The *NET Bible* translates this verse differently from any translations I've studied. According to the NET translators, Ruth uncovered more than Boaz's feet: "When he gets ready to go to sleep, take careful notice of the place where he lies down. Then go, uncover his <u>legs,</u> and lie down beside him. He will tell you what you should do." (Ruth 3:4 NET)

12. What did Ruth "uncover" according to the NET translation?

13. Read Daniel 10:5–6. This is a vision of Jesus. What part of his body was like bronze?

This Scripture passage is the defining reason for the NET translators' word choice. The Hebrew word is the same in the Ruth and Daniel passages.

> "Some define the noun מַרְגְּלֹת *(margÿlot)* as "the place for the feet" . . . but in Daniel 10:6 the word refers to the legs, or "region of the legs." For this reason "legs" or "lower body" is the preferred translation . . . Because "foot" is sometimes used euphemistically for the genitals, some feel that Ruth uncovered Boaz's genitals . . . Ruth and Boaz did not actually have a sexual encounter at the threshing floor, there is no doubt that Ruth's actions are symbolic and constitute a marriage proposal."[1]

Shocking? A puritanical upbringing may cause us discomfort with this scene. I've read commentary that explains this Scripture passage by comparing it with an ancient East custom where servants lay at their master's feet. But the servants weren't proposing marriage when they slept there. This wasn't a marriage custom in the Bible—lying at a man's feet. But having sex was. Read this commentary from Deffinbaugh:

> "When it comes to our text, some interpreters wish to persuade the reader that there was a common cultural practice underlying the actions which Naomi directed and Ruth carried out. But the reality is that we see no such practice in the Bible—anywhere! Thus, I take the text at face

value. I do not believe that there is some unique cultural interpretation here. . . . Remember that marriage was not consummated by the declaration of a preacher, or elder; marriage was consummated by the sexual union of a man and a woman. Once a marriage was consummated in the marriage bed, there was no easy way out. Ask Jacob about that. So, Naomi's plan was to coax Boaz to become the family redeemer by having sex with Ruth (under the influence of wine). And once that union was consummated, there was no turning back."[2]

14. Read Ruth 3:3–4 again. What is the last thing Naomi said to Ruth concerning Boaz?

This was a marriage proposal. Whether we want to believe Ruth uncovered his feet and lay at them or that she uncovered more than that and snuggled up close, either way, she proposed. The rest was up to Boaz. Thank goodness he was a gentleman.

Connecting with other Scripture

15. Read Hebrews 4:12–13. Is anything hidden from God?

16. What judges the attitude of our hearts?

"Nothing in all creation is hidden from God's sight. Everything is uncovered and laid bare before the eyes of him to whom we must give an account" (Hebrews 4:13 NIV).

17. What is "uncovered and laid bare" before the eyes of God?

Everything. Everything. Everything.

"And no creature is hidden from his sight, but all are <u>naked</u>¹¹³¹ and exposed to the eyes of him to whom we must give an account." (Hebrews 4:13)

18. Look up **1131** in the New Testament Dictionary in the back of this book. What does this term mean with respect to the body?

19. The word "uncovered" doesn't hold the connotations of "naked." How does it make you feel to think of standing figuratively "naked" before God?

20. Read John 8:3–11. Explain this story in your own words.

Movies depict this scene with the woman wrapped in nothing but a sheet as if she were actually, that very minute, caught in the act and dragged to the temple courts to receive her judgment.

Whether or not she was literally naked, I'm sure she felt that way—her sin uncovered and laid bare for all to see. Vulnerable. There she stood, uncovered, in front of Jesus.

21. What was Jesus' brilliant response to the Pharisee's question?

22. Did anyone throw a stone at her? Did Jesus condemn her?

23. Go back and read Hebrews 4:14–16. Why can we approach the throne of God with confidence despite our naked sin?

Ruth trusted Naomi, but I think she trusted Boaz even more. She'd received his protection, provision, and grace during the harvest. She had nothing to fear the night she made herself vulnerable to him. He understood her. His momma was once a foreigner, too.

Bringing the treasure home to our hearts

What pieces of your heart do you try to keep undercover for no one to see? Sin thrives in darkness. Wounds fester and roots grow deeper. Write down any sin, wound, or struggle you want to uncover, *gâlâh*, before God. If you don't trust me, can you trust Jesus?

Let's pray together

"Dear God, make us vulnerable to you. We can't hide anything anyway, but we try. Help us trust you so we might come before your throne *gâlâh* (gaw-law), exposed, nothing covered up, vulnerable to the living, loving God who died for us that we might live. You understand us. Thank you for Jesus. Amen."

How Are You with Commands?

Tsâvâh (tsaw-vaw´)

RUTH 3:5–6

Though my Chinese-American husband was raised next door to his grandparents, who kept Chinese traditions, none of his four sisters or he continues those cultural traditions with their own families. They are Americanized through and through. When we first married I described him as my six foot four Chinese California boy. I didn't experience cultural differences between us. But five years into our marriage, I understood that Mike's culture did influence him in the way he spoke to our children. It wasn't always as gentle as my parents were to me.

I realized the differences in our upbringing when my mother-in-law scolded me in her kitchen for not using the correct serving spoon for the Jell-O salad. Her reprimand didn't sit well with me. My family always used the serving spoon I'd chosen. It was smaller, but we never made a big deal about it. I confess, after trying to help that day, I promised myself I wouldn't set foot in that kitchen again. I didn't like her demanding tone.

Mike's family barked orders to each other (or it sounded that way to me.) I was from a soft-spoken, polite, Southern family. We never demanded. I always ended a request with "please." His family didn't. They were lovely people. A good family. But that day I realized their culture was different from mine, and that affected the way they spoke to each other.

But truthfully, though a shock at first, I now appreciate their straightforward requests and demands. My way doesn't always get the attention needed. My kids often took advantage of my kinder approach.

I'm still working on it. But I used to say, "Drew, would you like to take the trash out for me, please?" It really wasn't a query. It was a command disguised as a polite question. But there were many times when my kids would say, "Naaaa . . . I really don't want to right now." At which I would then rephrase my question into a crescendo-ing command, "Take. Out. The. Trash!"

I learned the beauty of *tsâvâh*.

Digging for treasure

1. Read Ruth 3:5. How did Ruth respond to Naomi's bold directions?

2. How would you respond?

3. Do you think Naomi's tone was sweet or demanding?

Let's look into the ancient text to try to hear her tone. Tone always helps me obey with a good attitude. That's why I always tried to be sweet when instructing my kids to do chores. (Sometimes I was *too* nice.)

> ". . . and did everything her mother-in-law <u>told</u> her to do." (Ruth 3:6 NIV)

"... and did just as her mother-in-law commanded[6680] her." (Ruth 3:6 ESV)

4. Look up **6680** in the Old Testament Dictionary in the back of this book. What part of this definition conveys the emotion behind Naomi's instructions? Was she giving Ruth an option?

Naomi was giving Ruth strict orders. And Ruth complies . . . mostly. In a couple of days we will see that she has her own plan.

How did you follow commands as a child? How well do you follow rules now? Are you a people pleaser or a rebel?

I'm a people pleaser working on not being one. I was the teacher's pet. I'm not bragging, just confessing. Funny, what I used to think was a strength, was actually a weakness. (All strengths can be.) People pleasers follow instructions blindly, too afraid to veer off course. Ruth is wiser.

Yesterday we tried to better understand Naomi's instructions and intentions. Today we hear her authoritative tone. For the final preparation of the following scenes, let's better understand the mood of the threshing floor. What kind of situation was Ruth about to walk into? Well . . . a party. The threshing floor became a place of celebration because the strenuous work of the harvest was completed.

5. Read Deuteronomy 16:13–17. What did God command?

He commanded them to celebrate. However, as do many parties, these celebrations sometimes got out of control.

6. Read Hosea 9:1. Where were the prostitutes?

7. What does Boaz command in Ruth 3:14?

So, maybe it wasn't strange for a woman to be there at night. We'll discuss this some more on Day 24. I wanted us to see this verse today to prove what kinds of things happened during such celebrations. But I love what Boaz does . . .

8. Read Ruth 3:14 again. Why does Boaz command such secrecy?

Be still my heart. He's protecting Ruth again. I love it.

Connecting with other Scripture

Jesus protects women in *his* presence, too. This is one of my favorites:

9. Read John 12:1–7. What did Mary do?

10. How did Judas react?

11. How did Jesus respond?

Isn't his response wonderful? "Jesus said, 'Leave her alone . . .'" (John 12:7).

Those words are powerful, but the Greek is even better. Here's the ancient word and its meanings from *The Complete Word Study Dictionary New Testament:*

"*Aphiēmi:* to send. To send forth or away, let go from oneself."

12. Rewrite Jesus' response incorporating these meanings. Does this new understanding of the Greek word change the meaning of his defense?

Not only did Jesus protect her, he recognized the importance of her presence at the party. What would it mean to have Jesus recognize and defend your attendance in a room?

How many of us feel invisible, uninvited?

We've sat as wallflowers at one too many junior high dances. We know what it feels like to be left out and unwanted. But the same Jesus who recognized the value of Mary's company recognizes ours.

He also recognizes our purpose. Though the naysayers belittled Mary's sacrifice, Jesus explained her purpose, which was prophetic and of deeper meaning than any man in the room could comprehend. Personally, I don't think Mary understood the significance of her actions, but that didn't stop her from fulfilling her purpose that night—giving the most extravagant gift she owned to prepare Messiah for death.

The next time you read the Gospels, watch how Jesus treated the women he encountered.

Boaz is a great representative of our Jesus.

Bringing the treasure home to our hearts

Have you experienced a time when someone—or God himself—protected you? Share your story.

Do you believe that Jesus desires your presence? Why?

I encourage you to do this exercise:

Imagine yourself as Mary of Bethany. Picture yourself walking into that dinner party with your perfumed oil in hand. Notice your heart beat. Are you afraid? Excited? Nervous? Jesus is reclining on the floor; his legs are bent with his feet toward his back. You kneel beside him. As he continues talking with one of the disciples, you begin to pour the oil on those precious, dusty feet. As you do, Jesus immediately stops talking and looks toward you. All eyes fall on you. There's a hush in the room.

Suddenly emotions overtake you. Wails erupt from the deepest places of your soul. Despite your greatest effort, the tears cannot be contained. Immense sorrow explodes out of you. You wipe his feet with your hair and kiss those feet that will soon be nailed to a cross. You want to sit there forever. He puts his hand on your head.

You can faintly hear someone complaining, but Jesus' voice hushes the room again. "Leave her alone. Let her stay. I value her presence . . . her purpose."

No hurry. Don't rush your time with Jesus. What is he telling you?

Let's pray together

"Holy Spirit, fill us so we will follow your leadings. Thank you, Jesus, for treating women with kindness and respect—command, *tsâvâh* (tsaw-vaw´) the naysayers, "*Aphiēmi* (af-ee´-ay-mee)!" Thank you for recognizing our presence and purpose. Reveal anything holding us back from fully trusting you—fully worshipping you. Amen."

More Than Startled

Chârad̲ (khaw-rad́)
RUTH 3:7–8

My daddy volunteered for the fire department in our town of 1,500 people. The small Texoma (on the border of Oklahoma and Texas) farming community was sprinkled with sirens positioned throughout the neighborhoods to warn of fire or tornadoes—a frequent threat, especially in the spring.

The sirens blew three times to warn of fire and alert the volunteers, and they rang four times if a funnel cloud threatened.

I often lay in bed in the middle of the night counting the siren rotations. Normally the phone rang if my dad needed to fight a fire, but I still counted the number of times those loud sirens blew. They were not a welcomed sound. No warm fuzzies are associated with this memory, only fear. I was scared to death of tornadoes.

One summer night I awakened to the loud warning. I lay in the dark counting each revolution of the siren. Though this was a common phenomenon, on this night my anxiety multiplied because I lay in bed with a cast on my leg. Surgery a few weeks earlier had impaired my ability to run. If we were going to leave, my dad would have to carry me.

My mind and heart sprinted . . . *What if he doesn't come get me in time? What if he can't carry me fast enough?*

I counted the rotating siren. *One. Two. Three . . . Four!*

I sat up in bed and began yelling, "HELP! Help me! Daddeeeeeee!"

Like most days and nights when the tornado warning blew, my parents simply got up, walked outside to ascertain the conditions, and came back inside to wait out the storm. Despite the many warnings, I honestly never remember running to our neighbor's storm-cellar, and this frightening night would be no different.

My dad crept into my room, assured me everything was okay, and instructed me to go back to sleep.

But I was *chârad*—terrified! Sleep could not be found. But neither could a tornado.

Digging for treasure

1. Read Ruth 3:7. Where did Boaz lie down after he "was in good spirits?"

2. Why would he choose this place to sleep?

We've learned this was a celebration time after the harvest, but threshing involved work—dangerous work done at night when thieves stole from the grain piles. Winnowing was an interesting process. This commentary explains:

> "The winnowing process is performed by throwing up the grain, after being trodden down, against the wind with a shovel. . . . The farmer usually remained all night in harvest-time on the threshing floor, not only for the protection of his valuable grain, but for the winnowing. That operation was performed in the evening to catch the breezes which blow after the close of a hot day, and which continue for most of the night. This duty at so important a season the master undertakes himself; and accordingly, in the simplicity of the ancient manners, Boaz, a person of

considerable wealth and high rank, laid himself down to sleep on the barn floor, at the end of the heap of barley he had been winnowing."[1]

Now that we understand winnowing, let's get back to the dark threshing floor.

3. Explain in your own words what Ruth did after Boaz lay down.

4. Read Ruth 3:8. According to your Bible, how did Boaz react when he woke up in the middle of the night?

"At midnight the man was startled[2729] and turned over, and behold, a woman lay at his feet!" (Ruth 3:8)

The ancient text is interesting. I've chuckled at some of the words translators have chosen to protect the idea of Ruth lying at Boaz's feet, and "startled" seems tame compared with its Hebrew counterpart. Read the definitions and see if you agree with me.

Look up **2729** in the Old Testament Dictionary in the back of this book and list five meanings of *chârad* that pertain to this scene.

5. How would you describe Boaz's reaction?

Well, one thing is for sure, Boaz wasn't in the habit of having strange women sleeping next to him.

6. How does your Bible describe Boaz's movement in verse 8 before he discovers a woman?

"It happened in the middle of the night that the man was startled and <u>bent forward</u> (*lāpat*); and behold, a woman was lying at his feet" (Ruth 3:8 NASB, addition mine).

This translation made me chuckle. The meaning of the Hebrew word they've translated as "bent forward" will explain my thoughts:

   lāpat: to twist, grasp, turn, grasp with a twisting motion[2]

These are other translations:

> ". . . and he <u>turned </u>and discovered a woman." (NIV)
> ". . . and turned over, and behold, a woman lay at his feet!" (ESV)

8. The words *bent over* are nowhere to be found in the meaning of *lāpat*, but twisting and turning are. So, what does this verb tell you? Where do you think she was lying? Was she at his feet or beside him?

The NET Bible, in accordance with what we studied yesterday, is more specific: "In the middle of the night he was startled and turned over. Now he saw a woman lying beside him!" (Ruth 3:8 NET)

Writers are taught to use exclamation points sparingly. But I do believe an exclamation mark fitting at the end of verse 8.

Can you recall a time when someone or something suddenly startled or terrified you?

Connecting with other Scripture

Many Bible stories tell of people being frightened by angels. My favorite is Gabriel's startling visit to Mary when he appeared to her in Nazareth.

9. Read Luke 1:26–30. What is Mary's reaction when Gabriel appears?

10. What does Gabriel tell her in Luke 1:30?

11. Was Mary troubled by Gabriel, or by something he said?

Gabriel's words frightened Mary. Usually an angel's presence terrified the person. Let's study his greeting to discover what troubled Mary.

12. What is Gabriel's greeting in Luke 1:28?

"And he came to her and said, 'Greetings, O <u>favored one</u>[5487], the Lord is with you!'"

The words "favored one" troubled Mary. If an angel of the Lord greeted me with these words I would be ecstatic, not afraid. When this happens in the Bible, when actions don't line up with the words, it's time to do some digging.

13. Look up **5487** in the New Testament Dictionary in the back of this book. This divine favor is only spoken of twice in the Bible. To whom has it been given? Where is the other Scripture passage?

14. Read Ephesians 1:3–6. List what God has done through Jesus.

> "... he predestined us for adoption as sons through Jesus Christ, according to the purpose of his will, to the praise of his glorious grace with which he has blessed [5487] us in the Beloved" (Ephesians 1:5–6).

According to *The Complete Word Study Dictionary New Testament*:

> "In *charitoō*[5487] there is not only the impartation of God's grace, but also the adoption of into God's family in the imparting of special favor in the distinction to *charizomai* (G5483), 'to give grace, to remit, to forgive.'"[3] (Emphasis mine.)

What does this favor do?

15. Read Ephesians 1:13–14. Whom do believers receive?

Come back to the scene with Mary and Gabriel. Mary was favored, *charitoō*. *Gabriel told her so.* Perhaps this is a stretch, but I view *charitoō*, this working favor or grace, as instantaneously life-changing. *Charitoō* is a verb. Mary's life was changed forever as Messiah grew in her womb. Our lives change the minute we receive the life of the Holy Spirit of Jesus inside us, and we're adopted at that moment into God's family just as Mary was chosen in a moment to be God's vessel to bring the Christ child into the world. Simply put, when we are *charitoō* our identity changes. We are never the same.

16. Read Luke 1:31–33. What is your favorite part of Gabriel's prophecy about Jesus?

17. Read Luke 1:34–37. What is the sign Gabriel gives Mary?

18. According to Luke 1:37, what is impossible with God?

Some of us need to write Luke 1:37 on twenty index cards and tape them all over our house, in our car, on our desk, and on every mirror. Please hold on to this truth. Ruth and Naomi are perfect examples of the truth and power of Gabriel's proclamation. Two chapters ago their lives looked hopeless. Now Ruth is proposing to Boaz. God doesn't always do what we desire or need on our timetable or according to our game plan. But.

Nothing. Is. Impossible. With. God.

Please write that down.

20. According to Luke 1:38, how did Mary respond to Gabriel's call once she understood God's *charitoo* on her?

She held within her a servant's heart. Boaz did, too.

Bringing the treasure home to our hearts

Have you experienced a life-changing moment that scared you to death? What did you do? What happened? Do you believe God orchestrated the event?

Let's pray together

"Dear God, 'Elōhiym (el-o-heem), Shadday (sha-dah´-ee), Sovereign Creator, calm our fears when we are *chârad̪* (khaw-rad´). Make us your servants. Grant us your life-changing *charitoo* (khar-ee-to´-o), enabling us to follow your call. Our lives are not our own. We are yours. Amen."

The Corner of His Garment

Gâàl (gaw-al´)

RUTH 3:9

My soldier husband was deployed to a peacekeeping mission in Kosovo while we lived in Germany. The deployment was scheduled to last six months.

The first weeks of separation during a military deployment are the hardest, but after a while you find a routine, or "battle rhythm," as I like to call it. Months into Mike's absence I found my rhythm. I was doing great. Every day I appreciated my husband more and more realizing all he did for our family, but more importantly, every day it became increasingly clearer that God himself was my source. All other blessings (husband, children, home) were just icing on the cake. I learned to lean on Jesus alone.

A chapel women's ministry became my "job." I served on the leadership team, which afforded me the chance to teach Bible studies and speak. When Lauren and Stephen were in school and baby Drew took a nap, I would spread my Bible study all over the dining room table, light a candle, pour some coffee, and spend hours with the Lord—well, at least an hour, depending on Drew's nap and whether I fell asleep trying to get him to sleep.

My kids were young—ages nine, seven, and three. I was a busy momma. Busyness didn't allow time for sadness, but one night at the end of a long day, I climbed into my empty bed. The darkness was heavy, the sleeping house lonely. I missed my man.

I whispered to the Lord, "I know you're my source and Mike is the icing on top, but Lord, I miss him. I can feel his arms around me when he's here, but I can't feel yours."

As I rolled over turning my face toward the wall, tears streamed down my cheeks. And invisible yet tangible arms wrapped around me. I closed my eyes and fell asleep literally in the arms of God. That night the Lord covered me with his presence, and my loneliness was *gâa'l. Redeeemed* by my Redeemer.

Digging for treasure

1. Read Ruth 3:9. How did Ruth introduce herself?

2. How did this differ from the way she was addressed earlier in the book of Ruth? (Ruth 2:2, 6, 21)

3. Do you see any significance in the lack of "Moabitess" in her name?

Ruth simply calls herself Boaz's servant, *Ruth.*

I like Liz Curtis Higgs's thoughts about this in her book, *The Girl's Still Got It.* Liz writes, "By sharing her name, Ruth also demonstrates how much she trusts Boaz. In ancient Israel, knowing someone's name gave you the power to control him or her. Doubly so, I'd say if you add the word "servant," as Ruth has."[1]

4. Do you remember what Naomi instructed Ruth to say after she uncovered Boaz?

Well, the best-made strategy doesn't always fall into place as planned. Naomi probably didn't foresee Boaz's fear when he awoke with a woman sleeping next to him. Maybe Ruth improvised a bit when Boaz seemed confused. She had to tell him who she was, but rather than asking him what to do, she gave him instruction. I love it. Ruth knew Boaz much better than Naomi knew him. She had spent months working in his fields with his servants. Servants always know their master well. I'm sure Ruth learned a lot about him as she gleaned the crops with the other servants.

5. What did Ruth instruct Boaz to do?

Some believe that Ruth started a marriage ritual that night because there are no other marriage proposals in the Bible like this one. There was a custom in medieval Jewish wedding ceremonies where the groom removed his prayer shawl to cover his bride, symbolizing his protection and care.[2]

Only one Scripture passage, written years *after* the book of Ruth, refers to this custom. This passage speaks of God and his Jerusalem bride.

6. Read Ezekiel 16:8. What did God's covering do for Jerusalem?

The imagery is beautiful. Many commentators do not know where Ruth the Moabitess learned this nontraditional request, but I love Liz Higgs's thoughts; I must quote her again: "I believe with all my heart that the Lord himself breathed the following words into Ruth and then gave her the courage to speak them: 'Spread the corner of your garment over me.'"[3]

7. I wonder if Ruth gleaned the meaning of these words while working in Boaz's field. Read Ruth 2:12. What are the similarities of Boaz's words and Ruth's request?

"Corner of garment" and "wings" are translated from the same Hebrew word. *Kānāp̄* holds both meanings:

> "*Kānāp̄*: a common noun for a wing, the skirt or corner of a garment.
> It is the basic sense of 'to cover'; an attached extremity. It indicates the
> wings of various birds or winged creatures in general . . ." (CWSDOT)

Did Boaz's words spoken in Chapter 2 become reality to Ruth as she trusted YHWH and found favor, protection, and provision? Did she discover that which faith in the Hebrew God afforded those who believed? Did she transfer her understanding of the provision of God (while under his wings—trusting him) to her kinsman-redeemer, whose covering she desperately needed for redemption? "The LORD repay you for what you have done, and a full reward be given you by the LORD, the God of Israel, under whose wings you have come to take refuge!" (Ruth 2:12)

If Boaz had only known how his blessing to Ruth would play out later. I'm sure he had no idea that one day he himself would be her reward and her literal covering.

8. What did Ruth inform Boaz he was? (Ruth 3:9)

Yes, he was a kinsman-redeemer.

9. Do you remember this word in Hebrew? Look up **1350** in the Old Testament Dictionary in the back of this book to refresh your memory. According to the definition, how does this word apply to Ruth 3:13?

10. What were "the duties of relationship" here? (Answer found in the beginning of the definition of **1350**).

Boaz was a kinsman-redeemer. The DNA in his blood made him a candidate to redeem Ruth. He wasn't Mahlon's brother, but he came from the same family line. That made him responsible according to the Law.

Have you visualized the scene?

Ruth had tiptoed toward the sleeping Boaz. As she removed his blanket or cloak covering his legs she held her breath. She didn't want to wake him yet. Slowly she positioned herself right next to him—close enough for his blanket or cloak to reach. When he awoke, she requested that he cover her. If he did, I picture the beloved Ruth and Boaz under the covers together. Though not one commentator, including myself, believes anything happened sexually, the scene is symbolic of the marriage bed.

There's just something about that covering. Something about sharing the sheets.

Connecting with other Scripture

11. Read Ezekiel 16:8 again. What did the Lord cover with the corner of his garment?

12. Look up **6172** in the Old Testament Dictionary. What are the literal and figurative meanings?

13. What does *ervâh* symbolize to you?

"Vulnerable." That's what I think of when I think of *ervâh*. Everything showing. Nothing hidden. Completely vulnerable to the Lord.

14. Is it good to be naked/vulnerable before God? Why or why not?

15. What did the Lord do after he covered Jerusalem?

16. What happened after they entered into a covenant?

". . . and you will become mine" (Ezekiel 16:8).

I love those words.

17. What feelings do those words evoke in you? It may be something totally different than what I feel. That's the most wonderful part about this breathing document called the Bible. It speaks to us right where we need it to.

All this covering reminds me of another covering. This one is done by Jesus.

18. Read Romans 4:4–7. Who is blessed?

19. Read Revelation 5:9–10. With what did Jesus, our *Gâál*, purchase men for God?

We can't wrap our minds around it. But the blood of Jesus covers our shame and purchases us—redeems us into the family of God.

Ruth told Boaz to cover her. Because of the Ezekiel verse, I'm tempted to wonder how *ervâh* she was. There's no indication that she wore no clothes, but she needed to be covered. (Though she could've asked to be covered even fully dressed.) Whether or not she was literally *ervâh,* there is no doubt she positioned herself in a vulnerable place—it could've been a shameful situation. But she could dare to make this bold move because she trusted Boaz.

Bringing the treasure home to our hearts

Have you lay *ervâh* before the Lord? You can take that question as literally or as figuratively as you like. Again, have you lain *ervâh* next to him? Vulnerable. All shame exposed. Nothing hidden, a naked soul before Jesus. He is trustworthy.

Have you told Jesus you want his covering? Remember, when you tell him this, it involves a covenant. A marriage. If you are already married, now you have two husbands—Jesus and your current husband. It's okay. A marriage to Jesus will only benefit your earthly one.

Write a prayer to Jesus. Allow yourself to come *ervâh* before him. Be vulnerable. Hide nothing. Tell him you desperately need and want his covering. If you've been covered by Christ for many years, it's always good to renew your vows.

Let's pray together

"Jesus, here we are. We're coming to you *ervâh* (er-vaw´). Please be our *Gâa'l* (gaw-al´). Cover us. Amen."

A Woman of *Hutspa!*

Chayil (khah´-yil)

RUTH 3:10–12

D o you know her? She's perfect . . . PERFECT!

In case you don't know her, let me introduce you:

"An excellent wife who can find? She is far more precious than jewels. The heart of her husband trusts in her, and he will have no lack of gain. She does him good, and not harm, all the days of her life. She seeks wool and flax, and works with willing hands. She is like the ships of the merchant; she brings her food from afar. She rises while it is yet night and provides food for her household and portions for her maidens. She considers a field and buys it; with the fruit of her hands she plants a vineyard. She dresses herself with strength and makes her arms strong. She perceives that her merchandise is profitable. Her lamp does not go out at night. She puts her hands to the distaff, and her hands hold the spindle. She opens her hand to the poor and reaches out her hands to the needy. She is not afraid of snow for her household, for all her household are clothed in scarlet. She makes bed coverings for herself; her clothing is fine linen and purple. Her husband is known in the gates when he sits among the elders of the land. She makes linen garments and sells them; she delivers sashes to the merchant. Strength and dignity are her clothing, and she laughs at the time to come. She opens her mouth with wisdom, and the teaching of kindness is on her tongue. She looks well to the ways of her household and does not eat the bread of idleness. Her children rise up and call her blessed; her husband also, and he praises her: 'Many women have done excellently, but you surpass them all.'" (Proverbs 31:10–29)

She was the original Wonder Woman.

If I compare myself to her, I fail miserably. I don't measure up.

I tried to sew when my kids were little. I was terrible at it. I sewed my thumb one day. Thankfully the needle just went through the very tip, and I pulled it out quickly.

I stopped sewing when my daughter told me she felt like a taco in her Christmas dress that I had made to match mine.

Trees and weeds grow in my dilapidated garden boxes.

The only flax I select is in a package from Costco.

I don't know what a distaff is, much less how to work with a spindle.

I do try to lend a hand to the needy, but I often feel guilty that I'm not helping enough.

I don't make coverings for my bed. I buy mine at Walmart, but I do make my bed—most days. Does that count?

My children arise and call me "Momma."

And I turn the lights off when I go to bed.

The Proverbs 31 woman makes me tired. I don't have her *chayil*, her strength and virtue. But the Bible wasn't written to make us feel less than others, so I know I need to study this Hebrew word that describes her. Boaz used *chayil* to describe Ruth, too. Maybe there is hope for us, my friends.

Digging for treasure

1. Read Ruth 3:10. What did Boaz say to Ruth?

2. When have we heard him say these words?

3. Did he think badly of her for what she did? How do you know?

4. According to what we've learned in previous lessons, what do you think is the Hebrew counterpart for this "kindness"?

Yes, he viewed her marriage proposal as *chêsêd*.

5. Why did Boaz see her actions as *chêsêd?*

What a humble man! Despite his wealth and "good catch" characteristics, he saw beyond the initial wedding proposal as a way for Ruth to benefit Naomi. He viewed her proposal as sacrificial.

It makes you wonder how old he really was. If he was eighty as some commentators believe, this would've been a definite sacrifice on Ruth's part—at least as seen through our modern-day filters. Marriage is so very different now. Marrying for love is the only marriage we endorse. But marriage back then was often a business transaction.

6. What does Boaz tell Ruth in the first sentence of Ruth 3:11?

Stop for a minute. These words tell us something very important. In Day 20 we witnessed Boaz's fright/fear. But now he instructed *her* not to be afraid.

7. What does this tell you about the situation in which Ruth dared to place herself?

8. Why would she be afraid?

Well, it was dark. She was lying next to an "uncovered" man. She proposed to him rather than waiting for him to propose to her. Her reputation was on the line. Actually, if this didn't go well, Naomi would be affected, too. If this scheme deteriorated, Ruth would lose the best gig she and Naomi had to support and feed them. If she botched her relationship with Boaz, she lost her food source. She could lose his favor.

But she didn't.

9. Read all of Ruth 3:11. What reason did Boaz give for promising he would do what she asked?

Notice the different translations:

> ". . . you are a woman of *noble character.*" (NIV)
> ". . . you are a *worthy* woman." (ESV)
> ". . . you are a *worthy* woman." (NET)
> ". . . you are a woman *of good character.*" (CJB)

10. Go back to Ruth 2:1. The narrator introduces Boaz. How was he described?

The author of Ruth employed the same Hebrew word to describe Ruth and Boaz. Ruth started as a "Moabitess," but she transformed right before the villagers' eyes. Her native country was no longer her identity—only her good heart identified her. Now both Ruth and Boaz are known for their *chayil*. We studied this word on Day 2, but let's look at it again.

11. Look up **2428** in the Old Testament Dictionary in the back of this book. Write down the main words that describe this term.

> ". . . for all my fellow townsmen know that you are a *worthy woman*." (Ruth 3:11)

12. How would you translate the latter part of Ruth 3:11? Do you agree with the translations above or would you choose another word? Write down how you translate this verse according to the definitions you've read.

When a translator interprets a word, he or she only chooses one word out of the possible meanings. I always want to combine them. But a translator must consider the context of the sentence to find the correct counterpart. I do believe Ruth was extremely *strong*. She carried the equivalent of eleven two-liter soda bottles back home after her first day working in Boaz's field. She wasn't wealthy financially, but she was definitely *able* and filled with *substance*, or *hutspa*! Good audacity. I believe she would've made a *valiant warrior* if she found herself on a battlefield. But the context of this sentence does not pertain to war but rather her reputation. So Boaz said,

> ". . . thou art a *virtuous* woman." (KJV)

13. Look up the word *virtue* and write down the definition(s).

The first definition of *virtue* in my college dictionary is: "general moral excellence; right action and thinking; goodness or morality."

But as I scrolled down through the definitions, I was amazed when I read the sixth entry:

"[Now Rare] manly quality; strength, courage—by (or in) virtue of, because of; on the grounds of—*make a virtue of necessity to do or accept with an agreeable or positive attitude that which must be done or accepted anyway*" (Webster, emphasis mine).

14. Underline the words in the definition above that correlate with the meaning of the Hebrew word *chayil*.

Isn't that interesting? Our modern minds automatically think of morality when we hear the word *virtue*, but I find it fascinating that virtue is related to strength. And virtue correlates with "to do or accept with an agreeable or positive attitude that which must be done or accepted anyway."

Was this the kind of *virtuous* or *worthy woman* Boaz called Ruth? Do you think his word meant, "We know you're a woman who will do what needs to be done"? Did this mean Boaz knew if he didn't do as she asked she'd find someone else or at least take off his sandal and spit in his face?

15. Gleaning from what we've just unearthed, what is a new understanding of Boaz's words to Ruth? Was he talking about morality or tenacity (or both)?

16. Read Ruth 3:12. How does Boaz prove his virtue with our new understanding of this word?

That's right. Even though Boaz could've embraced the moment, taking Ruth as his wife, he knew she wasn't his to take—yet. He lived his life by the rules. There were a few formalities requiring attention, a slight hiccup in Naomi and Ruth's plan. But Boaz promised he would do what needed to be done. Ruth would be redeemed by somebody before the day ended.

Connecting with other Scripture

17. Read Proverbs 31:10. How does your translation describe a wife who is worth more than rubies?

- "A wife of *noble character* . . ." (NIV)
- "An *excellent* wife . . ." (ESV)
- ". . . a *capable* wife. . . ." (CJB, JSB [*Jewish Study Bible*])

18. Can you guess the Hebrew counterpart for the words *noble, excellent,* and *capable*?

19. Glance through Proverbs 31:10–31 again. List the characteristics of this woman that reveal the meaning of *chayil* as we've studied today?

20. Which of her characteristics do you most admire?

21. Do you share any of her qualities?

22. If you've been a Christian for a long time and are familiar with the Proverbs 31 woman, has she been a blessing to you or a burden—something you can't live up to? Why?

Some women love her. I've never really liked her very much. We sink in the quicksand of comparison, but we grow wings in the presence of camaraderie. If you read a Scripture passage and are burdened by it, please study and pray until you find your wings again. God's conviction never burdens, it always brings freedom and life. The Enemy wants us to believe we aren't good enough—we don't measure up.

Rather than trying to live up to everything the Proverbs 31 woman does, can you read this as a testament to the value of women? She wasn't stuck barefoot and pregnant in the kitchen. She thrived as a businesswoman who took care of her family.

God's Word does not burden.

23. Read Matthew 11:28. Describe Jesus' yoke.

Every rabbi presented his own teaching, or "yoke." The Pharisees' yoke was burdensome to the people. They could never measure up to it. But Jesus didn't teach a bunch of dos and don'ts.

24. Read Mark 12:28–31. What are the greatest commandments?

25. How would your life change if you only focused on these two commandments?

Do you see that this is how Ruth lived?

Bringing the treasure home to our hearts

Self-worth. It's something I've struggled with through my years as a stay-at-home mom. The world puts value on money. Salaries. At least that is one way of measuring one's value. Keeping my house clean, cooking every night, picking up toys an hour after picking up the same toys, cleaning spit-up off my shirt. Those were my days. I didn't look like the virtuous Proverbs woman—or the valuable career woman.

I had to go to Jesus for my strength, virtue, and value.

What about you? Are you trying to measure up? Do you long to be *chayil*? Are you burdened by what the world says you should be or even . . . what the church says? Are you simply burdened by comparing yourself with other women? Share your thoughts.

If I understand what we uncovered today, a woman of *chayil* is a woman who simply has strength to do what she knows needs to be done for the day. I know that some days we'll need more strength than others. But that's where prayer and Jesus come in.

Let's pray together

"Oh, Jesus, give us the *chayil* (khah´-yil) of Ruth. Don't let us be burdened by anything outside of your will for us today. Fill us with your Spirit—your strength to do whatever we need to do no matter how hard or strange. Help us take off all yokes that weigh us down. Blind us to comparison; let us only see the areas of camaraderie with all women, both present and biblical. Thank you for loving us. Help us love. Amen."

Life in the Promise

Chay (khah'ee)
RUTH 3:12–15

We planned a November wedding, but Saddam Hussein interfered.

"I'm going to the desert," Mike told me over the phone. "We either need to move up the wedding or wait until I get back."

Panic.

This was the love of my life, the man I had waited for! My prince in army boots and camouflage. What was I going to do? My fiancé's battalion would soon be deployed to fight a war.

I drove my parents crazy, calling daily for advice. Should we elope? Plan a big wedding in two weeks? Or wait?

I'd always dreamed of a big wedding, as most little girls do. But I'd dreamed of a big wedding because my parents had eloped—I grew up without their wedding pictures, and I wanted my children to have a wedding album to look through as they grew. Because my parents eloped, my mom encouraged me to have the big wedding because she knew only too well how life takes over and the formal wedding never happens if it's not done the first time. So . . . we planned a big wedding in two weeks.

No invitations sent.

No tough decisions concerning flowers or venue, whatever we found sufficed. No rehearsal or rehearsal dinner. One of my bridesmaids would fly in from California only an hour before the wedding.

You'll learn in the introduction to Day 24 that I purchased my wedding gown before I received the ring. Wasn't that a good thing! But bridesmaids' dresses and a flower girl's dress and a wedding cake needed to be made. Proverbs 31 women stepped up to the task to make my dream come true.

We married at eight o'clock on a Friday night—two weeks after we made the decision to move our wedding up three months. Our preacher invited the congregation. I'll never forget his words: "Mike Lee is sitting on a duffel bag waiting to deploy. You're all invited to the wedding." More than two hundred people attended including soldiers in dress blues and eighth-grade cheerleaders in their new uniforms.

A few days before that crazy wedding a friend confided in me her reservations about my decision to marry before my soldier left for battle.

"What if he gets injured or killed?" she asked. "I wouldn't marry a man going to war. It's too risky."

I knew her intentions were good. But her words were incapable of persuading my heart.

As surely as I *chay*—lived—I was not letting this man go. Whether he came back alive uninjured or not, I had to be married to Mike Lee if only for a few days.

Digging for treasure

1. Read Ruth 3:12–13. What does Boaz tell Ruth in this passage?

2. Do you think Ruth's heart sank when he told her there was another kinsman-redeemer? If you were Ruth, what would you think or feel?

Her plans had worked so well up to this point.

3. Have you found yourself in a situation that didn't go as planned? What did you do?

I try to remain calm, but my knee-jerk reaction is always to make an S.O.S. phone call to my prayer-buddy, though I know I need to pray to the Lord first. My stomach knots up, and my head pounds from thoughts running a thousand laps around my brain. There's no shutting it off. If I had been Ruth lying there on that cold threshing floor, I wouldn't have slept a wink. What about you?

But Boaz made a promise that would have calmed my fears.

4. Read Ruth 3:13. What does Boaz promise?

5. Why would this promise make Ruth's heart flutter?

Oh, Boaz, we like you so much. What a great guy! He follows the rules, but he promises to rise up to the occasion and do his part if the other guy bails. If I were Ruth, I would be praying under my breath for the other kinsman to renounce his duty. (I wonder if she was.)

Boaz's faithful words were endearing, but I want us to see the power and tradition behind his proclamation. "But if he is not willing to redeem you, then, as the LORD lives,[2416] I will redeem you" (Ruth 3:13b).

6. Look up **2416** in the Old Testament Dictionary in the back of this book. Write down the Hebrew word. Is the translation the same as the meaning?

"As surely as the Lord lives" is translated from יְהֹוָה *(YWHW)* חַי *(chay)* (CWSDOT).

Chay does mean "live," but it's a word that played a very important role in the Old Testament, as explained by editor Spiros Zodhiates:

> "Used in oaths and exclamations, in the sense of 'as surely as I [or you] live.' The certainty of God's promises, instructions, and judgments are signified by His prefacing comment, 'As surely as I live.' The OT places a high value on life. God is the Source of life and the Lord of life."[1]

7. This important Hebrew word is used in Numbers 14:21–24. Read this passage and explain the seriousness of God's oath.

8. Read Isaiah 49:18–19. What does God promise?

Do you hear the history, faith, and power of this word, *chay*, as this promise left Boaz's lips? I think this is my favorite quality of Boaz, his faith. Actually, his faith is what makes him who he is, isn't it? It's not the wealth or status that draws me to Boaz; it's his faith in YWHW.

9. What does your Bible translation say Boaz will do in Ruth 3:13?

> "But if he is not willing to redeem you, then, as surely as the Lord lives I will <u>redeem</u>[1350] you" (Ruth 3:13b).

Can you guess the one Hebrew counterpart without looking in the Old Testament Dictionary in the back of this book?

You got it. *Gâa'l.*

"And now it is true that I am a redeemer. Yet there is a redeemer nearer than I. Remain tonight, and in the morning, if he will redeem you, good; let him do it. But if he is not willing to redeem you, then, as the LORD lives, I will redeem you. Lie down until the morning" (Ruth 3:12–13).

How many times is the word "redeem(er)" used in this passage?

Repetition indicates an important point. Is the point made?

Yes. One way or the other, Ruth will be redeemed.

10. What does Boaz instruct Ruth to do?

11. Why would he insist she stay until morning?

Fun Fact: I was privileged to tour Israel with a close friend (my neighbor in Germany). Every morning my friend would say, "Boker Tôb!" As I write the words I can still hear her giggle after her cheery greeting. My brain and foreign languages don't connect. I was still stuck on the German greeting, "Guten morgen!" (Good morning). This would always be my less-than-intelligent reply. Now, years away from Germany and after a few years of studying limited Hebrew, I embrace this Hebrew greeting.

We studied the word *Tôb* (good) on Day 15. From my rambling above, can you ascertain the Hebrew word for "morning"?

You're so smart. Yes, the Hebrew counterpart is *Boker.* Now you can greet your family or roommates in a different language tomorrow morning!

Back to Ruth.

12. As much as I hate to bring this up, do you think Ruth simply lay there that night or do you think there was some action under the covers? Why?

Personally, I don't think anything sexual happened. Boaz was such a stickler for the rules. Nothing happened physically between the two. But I don't believe Ruth got a wink of sleep. Her eyes were probably wide open the entire night because . . .

13. Read Ruth 3:14 and explain when Ruth got up.

Only a soft blue in the sky promised the coming sun, but it was all Ruth needed to climb out from the blanket and tiptoe out. I wonder if she was hoping not to wake Boaz. But he probably didn't go back to sleep either. Can't you just see both of them lying perfectly still, trying not to touch, their eyes wide open staring into the darkness? The morning probably could not come fast enough for either Ruth or Boaz.

14. Read Ruth 3:14 again. What instruction did Boaz give the other men?

I grew up believing that secrets were bad. Maybe that's why I never could keep one. But are there times when secrets are necessary?

If so, this is one of those times. Her protection requires this secret. Boaz would go to the "city hall" as soon as the sun rose. He had some redeeming to do . . . as surely as he lives—*chay*.

Connecting with other Scripture

There was another lady in the Bible who needed to be redeemed. In fact, I believe she was passed down through five levirate marriages. Unless you are Elizabeth Taylor, why would any woman choose to be married to five men? When Jesus met her she lived with a man not her husband. Every commentary I've read paints this woman as loose and sinful. When I read it, I see a woman rejected by five men and living with one who didn't love her enough to marry her. But an eternal Redeemer specifically stopped at the well one day at just the right time to meet her.

15. Read John 4:4–15. What does Jesus ask of the woman?

16. What does he promise her?

17. Read John 4:16–17. Does Jesus rebuke her or tell her to stop sinning?

No rebuke. No shame. Just truth.

18. Why do you think Jesus brought this truth to light?

I wonder if Jesus wanted her to know that he knew her. He *knew* all about her life, her heartache, her shame, yet this Rabbi chose to speak to her.

19. Read Deuteronomy 24:1–4. In what circumstances could a man divorce a woman?

The Hebrew word is *ervâh*[6172]. We studied this word on Day 21. Do you remember the literal and figurative meanings? Take a quick look in the Old Testament Dictionary in the back of this book and jot down the meanings for reference to answer the next questions.

19. Incorporating the figurative meanings of this Hebrew word, in what cases could a husband divorce his wife?

A man could divorce his wife if he found something wrong with her . . . a defect . . . a handicap.

20. What "handicap" or "defect" could a woman have that was only discovered after marriage? What was one of the most important things to biblical families?

After studying the law and understanding the meaning of *ervâh*, my heart breaks for this woman. Not only rejected by five husbands, she held another shame in her heart. What if the husbands divorced her because she couldn't conceive? This could be the reason she gathered water at the well at noon. Perhaps she avoided the early morning gathering of mothers and children—a painful place for a childless woman.

21. According to the Deuteronomy passage, could a former husband remarry her if her husband died?

Could this be why the Samaritan woman lived with a man who wasn't her husband?

22. Does the Deuteronomy passage affect the way you now view the Samaritan woman? Describe her with your new filters.

I love Jesus. Just a small part of a day in his presence redeemed this woman for eternity. She was still husband-less, no baby in her arms, but a little bit of time with the Living Water filled her to overflowing. They talked about worship and faith and then she proclaimed her trust in the coming Messiah. At that point Jesus told her, "I who speak to you am he" (John 4:26).

23. Read John 4:27–28. What did the woman once shamed do?

24. Read John 4:39–42. What happened after she told the townspeople? Why did they believe?

25. Had her life been redeemed?

Absolutely. Her life had not changed, but her heart had. Jesus gave her a purpose that day. He made her the first Samaritan evangelist. She no longer hid at the well by herself in the middle of the day when nobody would be there; she ran . . . she ran . . . she ran to tell the people who had once shamed her and mocked her. She ran to tell them to come see the Messiah.

There's one more thing I don't want us to miss in this story.

26. Read John 4:25. What does she tell Jesus?

27. What does this tell you about her?

It tells me she was expecting Messiah. She desperately watched for him. Her desperation intensified her faith. She needed a Savior.

Desperation can be a good thing.

Look where it put Ruth.

28. How are Jesus and Boaz similar?

Bringing the treasure home to our heart

We've gone all over the map with this lesson. What spoke to your heart?

Let's pray together

"Jesus, as surely as you *chay* (khah'ee), you've chosen us, protected us, and done everything necessary to redeem us. Thank you for the desperate days when we need you. Thank you that you are kind, gentle, trustworthy, and that after we've spent time with you, we're changed, given hope, and given a purpose for eternity. Amen."

Empty No More

Rēyqām (ray-kawm´)
RUTH 3:15–17

Restaurants and fast food choices were limited. Very limited. Grandfield boasted one greasy diner and Rhonda Rollins's daddy's Dairy Freeze. So, some Saturday nights our family of four piled into our blue Ford and drove to the nearest town, thirty minutes away, to enjoy a burger at a national chain drive-in. I loved going to Sonic.

On this night, silence pervaded the car as we gulped down our burgers and fries. But as I ate my hamburger, something didn't seem right. I looked more closely at my sandwich only to discover that the beef patty was missing. Only mayo, pickles and lettuce resided between the two buns in my hands. So, I did what any elementary age child would do. I began to inspect everyone else's meal—maybe they were eating bread sandwiches, too.

I peered over to my sister's hamburger. "You've got some," I observed out loud. I then scooted forward to inspect my dad's. Looking over his shoulder I spotted the beef. "You've got some, too," I continued.

I then slid toward my mom. But she stopped me mid-slide. "What are you doing?" she asked with a chuckle.

Holding my burger-less hamburger open, I explained, "I'm just looking to see if yours has meat. Mine doesn't!"

My burger was *rēyqām*, totally empty of what made it a hamburger.

Digging for treasure

1. Read Ruth 3:15. What did Boaz give Ruth?

2. Why do you think he did this?

The Hebrew text doesn't tell us how much grain Boaz gave her. There are many theories, but we've been studying Ruth for a long time now. We know Boaz well. We've also learned about the customs of the day. Let's use what we've learned to infer the amount of his grain gift.

3. Do you picture this gift as a small amount of grain or a lot? How big is the bundle on her back? Give your reasons for your answers.

Excellent! I don't know your answers; I just love the thought that you're discovering how to interpret meaning from Scripture based on other scriptural knowledge and the historical and character context.

I have read many theories in my research concerning the "six measures of barley." Some believe Boaz handed her six grains symbolizing the six descendants that would come through her womb.

4. Read Ruth 3:15 again and give your reasons why you do or don't agree with the six grains theory.

Did you disagree with this theory? If so, I'm with you. The six grains theory doesn't appear to fit the context of their movement. The commentary below better resonates with what we've learned about the culture and Boaz:

> ". . . the standard for the fellowship offering was set back in Genesis 18 by Abraham: Genesis 18:6 . . . Abraham hurried into the tent to Sarah, and said, 'Quickly, prepare three measures of fine flour, knead {it,} and make bread cakes.' Three measures of meal became the standard fellowship offering. By giving them six measures, Boaz was letting Naomi know that his fellowship with Ruth was also with her."[1]

5. Give reason(s) why you agree or disagree with this interpretation of Boaz's gift.

Reading the next verses will help. Let's keep on digging.

6. Read Ruth 3:16–17. How did Naomi address Ruth when the younger woman returned home?

I must show you something interesting from Ruth 3:16 that gives me cause to believe that tradition is often the reason for translation rather than the actual text.

> NIV: "How did it go, my daughter?"
> NET: "How did things turn out for you, my daughter?"
> ESV: "How did you fare, my daughter?

I noticed that all the translations added words to the ancient text. One Hebrew word is *miy:* "who, whose, whom." It is used in questions. (CWSDOT)

The next word in the Hebrew text is *bath,* which means "daughter." (CWSDOT)

7. Who am I to question many translators, but quite simply, when you look at the meaning of *miy* and *bath,* what do you think Naomi was asking?

I think she asked, "Whose daughter are you?" In other words, "Are you still mine or do you now belong to Boaz?" I discovered this new interpretation reading this commentary from Torah.org.:

> "A fascinating interpretation that is rich with psychological insight is suggested by Nachalas Yosef. Naomi asked Ruth, 'Do you still belong to me? Are you still mine or has Boaz taken you away from me? Whose are you now, my daughter, mine or his? . . . The six barleys were a message to Naomi, a message that committed Boaz to restore what she has lost . . ."[2]

Isn't that awesome? It agrees with my spirit; how about yours? We would never have found it if we hadn't dug deep into the text. Doesn't the Bible come to life and the characters grow more personal when we find treasures like this?

8. According to our new understanding of verse 16, why did Boaz give Ruth six measures of barley?

It's a promise. But it's not just a promise to Ruth; it's also a pledge to Naomi that Boaz will take care of her. (Remember this thought for the end of our lesson.)

9. Read 3:17. How does Ruth explain the big bag of barley she lugged home?

10. Hmmmm . . . did you catch that? "Don't go back to your mother-in-law . . . (finish the sentence.)

Empty. Again, we've added words for our culture. The Hebrew text is simply *rēyqām*.

"Don't go back to your mother-in-law *rēyqām*.

Rēyqām is an adverb meaning "empty-handed, empty." (CWSDOT)

11. Read Ruth 1:21. How had Naomi come back to Bethlehem?

This is the same Hebrew word.

I wonder if Naomi's spirit jumped when she heard Ruth give the reason for the barley. Certainly those hearing this story told down through generations would've caught the new hope and restoration God was bringing to the once broken, *rēyqām,* and bitter Naomi. Her emptiness was filling up. Don't forget that her "empty" began to change when her eyes turned off her problems and she began to help Ruth.

Connecting with other Scripture

12. Read Luke 6:38. The *measure* of barley in Ruth's story is not clear, but Jesus talks of measure, too. How does he speak of measure in this Scripture verse?

13. Have you experienced Jesus' promise of measure in your life? Explain.

14. Read Ephesians 3:16–19 and answer the following questions:

- From where will Christ strengthen us? (v. 16)

- Why does Paul pray for Christ to strengthen us? (v. 17)

- How does he pray for the Ephesians (and us) to be rooted? (v. 17b)

15. What does it mean to be rooted in something?

16. Why does Paul pray for them to be rooted in love?

17. What happens when we know the love of Christ?

18. Can we fathom this? What does it mean to be "filled to the measure of all the fullness of God"?

He is such a generous God! All that he is and has is ours to receive. I'm not talking about "stuff," girlfriends. We're talking about eternal and spiritual gifts—grace, love, forgiveness, wisdom, mercy, *chêsêd,* peace. We can never outgive our generous heavenly Papa.

19. Read Ephesians 1:13–14. Who were we "marked with" when we believed in Christ?

> ". . . who is the guarantee[728] of our inheritance until we acquire possession of it, to the praise of his glory."

20. Look up **728** in the New Testament Dictionary in the back of this book and write down your understanding of this word.

Did you write down the word "pledge"?

21. What was the promise, or pledge, Boaz gave Ruth?

Some believe Boaz gave Ruth sixty pounds of barley to carry home. My back hurts just thinking about it. I might have said, "Oh, you *really* don't have to, Boaz. That's too much, honey. Just give me part of it. That's all I need."

I know I would've said that! I do it all the time in the face of generosity. Why do we do that? Why is it difficult to say, "Thank you," and graciously accept the gift?

Ruth was good at this. She never refused Boaz's gifts, and it's a good thing because his gifts were never only for Ruth. His gifts blessed Naomi as well.

Bringing the treasure home to our hearts

Do you fight receiving support from others, whether financially or in some other way? Do you know why?

Do you resist accepting all that God has for you? Do you know why?

Would it make it easier to receive generosity from God and other people if you viewed the gifts given as blessings to share? Explain your thoughts.

Are you empty, *reyqām*? Do you believe that God wants to fill you?

All that God requires of us is to position ourselves in a place to receive, and truthfully, I think we must want it. Do you want all that God has for you? Let him know.

Let's pray together

"Jesus, how do we thank you? We have been so very *reyqām* (ray-kawm′), so empty, but you generously fill us with your Spirit—your generous pledge. We want more of you. Give us the full measure of you. Help us come to *know* you better. Enable us to receive your love, filled to overflowing, so we can spill your love out to all around us. Reveal yourself and your generous Spirit through Boaz as we continue this study. Amen."

No Rest

Kâlâh (kaw-law)

RUTH 3:18

We had dated five whole months. To my twenty-four-year-old self that was plenty of time. I met his parents. He met mine, and I knew he was the right one. I would've married him after our first date. We'd talked about marriage, and we picked out my engagement ring—I simply didn't have it yet.

The wedding date was set.

I taught school; therefore, I planned the wedding that summer, maximizing my days off so I wouldn't worry about our November wedding details once school resumed.

The bridesmaids' dress patterns and fabric were purchased. And my wedding gown hung beautifully in my closet.

But I didn't have my ring.

I grew impatient. *What was the hold-up?*

Perhaps the ring hasn't come yet, I reasoned.

Could he be changing his mind? I worried.

Weeks went by. No ring.

One Sunday, Mike and I planned to go to lunch after church, and just as every Sunday, I invited the entire singles group to go with us. As we ate lunch with our friends I couldn't understand why Mike acted so strange. He seemed angry.

After lunch we returned to my parents' house in a silent car.

What is his problem? I stewed.

About a half hour after we arrived back at my house, Mike called me outside. He sat me down on the back steps and he sat beside me. Turning toward me, his strong hand grasped mine, "There's a good reason why I was upset at lunch. You invited everyone."

"We always go out with the group," I replied, still clueless.

"Yes," he said, "but I planned to take you back to our restaurant where we had our first date and give you this."

My mouth dropped open.

Mike knelt on one knee holding a ring box in his hand. "I wanted to do this sooner, but I've been trying to reach your dad."

He then showed me the index card where he wrote the words to say asking permission to marry me.

He had tried for days. The index card was filled with "Good morning" scratched out and changed to "Good afternoon," which was scratched out and changed to "Good evening."

After many days, he finally reached my dad. It was clear by his index card that my sweet man could not rest until he properly asked for my hand in marriage, until the matter was finished—*kālāh.*

Digging for treasure

1. Read Ruth 3:18. Write Naomi's response to Ruth's news in your own words.

How are you when it comes to waiting?

The Hebrew word translated as "wait" is *yāšaḇ:* "A verb meaning 'to sit, to dwell, to inhabit, to endure, to stay.'" (CWSDOT)

2. Does the meaning of *yāšaḇ* give new definition to the word "wait"? How?

Is it hard for you to sit still or stay right where you are when you know big decisions are being made concerning your future? Do you think this was difficult for Ruth? Why?

3. Is Naomi worried or hopeful? How do you know?

4. How long must Ruth sit still?

"Sit still my daughter until you learn[3045] how the matter turns out."

5. Look up **3045** in The Old Testament Dictionary in the back of this study. What does it mean? When have we seen this word before?

We visited *yâḏa'* on Day 17. It means "to know." The next time someone tells you something you already know, you can say, "I *yâḏa'!*"

But I digress . . .

So, Ruth must *sit still* until she knows what?

> "Wait my daughter until you learn how the matter <u>turns out</u> . . ." (ESV)
> "Wait my daughter until you find out what <u>happens</u> . . ." (NIV)
> "Sit still my daughter until thou know how the matter <u>will fall</u> . . ." (KJV)

The underlined words are translations of the Hebrew word *nāpal*.

Read this definition: "To fall, be prostrate, be brought down . . . falling into the hands of the opponent or falling into the hands of another."[1]

Is there anything about this definition of *nāpal* that catches your eye?

Ruth must *sit still* waiting to know *whose hands she will fall into.*

Naomi would've had to sit on me. How scary would that be—waiting to know if you were to marry the man you liked or a stranger? I would've been tempted to run to the meeting to testify to my preference. What about you?

But Ruth and Naomi had done all they could do. Now it was up to Boaz. ". . . for the man will not rest but will <u>settle</u> the <u>matter</u> today." The ancient text brings life to this sentence, too.

"Matter" was translated from the Hebrew word *dābār*. This word means "word, speech, matter . . . <u>It signified spoken words or speech</u>." (CWSDOT)

I find this interesting. The word *dābār* can be used as "matter," but it's most often used for "speech" or "speaking." Boaz was going to *speak* to the kinsman-redeemer and the town elders. Hold that thought. There's one more word I want us to discover.

"Settled" has been translated from *kālāh,* which means "to be completed, finished, accomplished . . .."[2]

6. If Boaz is an archetype of Jesus, does the meaning of *kālāh* remind you of anything Jesus said on the cross?

7. Read John 19:30. What did Jesus say?

Is it just me, or do you find that powerful, too? Jesus completed our redemption just as Boaz will complete Ruth's and Naomi's. "The man will not rest until the conversation or matter is finished." (NIV)

8. Did Ruth or Naomi have any control at this point?

9. Did Boaz?

10. Who was ultimately in control now?

How do you feel when you aren't in control?

Connecting with other Scripture

11. Read Proverbs 3:5–6. According to your translation, how must you trust the Lord?

12. What can't be trusted or depended on?

13. Why?

Can you think of a time when you didn't understand why something happened, and you were upset, but years later you realized it had been a blessing? Please share.

14. Write down Proverbs 3:6 according to your translation.

"In all your <u>ways</u>[1870] <u>acknowledge</u>[3045] him, and he will make straight your paths."

Let's do some digging. If you aren't certain of the meaning of a Scripture passage, research the ancient words to better understand. Let's plow into the first half:

15. Find **1870** in the Old Testament Dictionary in the back of this study and jot down some of its meanings. Circle the one that fits best.

I chose the word "journey."

16. Find **3045** in your now most favorite place to dig, the Old Testament Dictionary in the back of this book, and write down some of the defining words that seem most applicable to this verse. Circle the one that surprises you.

We know this word. In the simplest of terms, what does it mean?

Yes, it means *to know* someone or something.

17. Using our new understanding of these words, how would you translate the first half of verse 6?

Let's do the second half. I think you'll be amazed.

    "... and he will make <u>straight</u>[3474] your <u>paths</u>.[734]"

18. What is the Hebrew word for **3474**? What are the two ways it can be used?

I find this definition from Spiros Zodhiates helpful:

> "... to be level, straight, upright, just, lawful; to make straight, declare right, approve; to be pleasing. Has two meanings: (a) making something straight or level; (b) ethically, an upright (moral) life ..."[3]

Which meaning did the author intend when he penned Proverbs 3:6b?

    "... and he will make <u>straight</u>[3474] your <u>paths</u>.[734]"

Studying the word "paths" will bring clarity.

19. Look up **734** in the Old Testament Dictionary. What are the literal and figurative meanings of this word?

"Often used figuratively, describing the way to righteousness or wickedness, the path leading to life or death."[4]

20. Do you think Proverbs 3:6 refers to literal paths or salvation?

21. Re-translate Proverbs 3:5–6 with your new understanding.

This is how I would translate the passage: "Trust in the Lord with all your heart, and don't try to understand your circumstances. On your life-journey always be familiar with him, know him, walk with him, and he will make you right with him, righteous, saved forever." I added a lot of words. Does yours look something like mine?

Let's go back to Ruth. She's reached a place in her life where she can't do anything more to improve her situation. The matter is completely out of her hands, but in a way, it's out of Boaz's control, too. Through the world's eyes, Ruth's fate lies in the hands of a man, but we know better. Who is ultimately in control of this situation? How do we know?

Yet there is no rest for Boaz until his job is *kālāh*—finished.

Bringing the treasure home to our heart

Have you experienced a life-altering situation you thought would never end? A situation that was out of your control that would change your life forever. What did you do while you waited for it to be resolved? Were you panicked? Frustrated? Angry? Or did you have peace as you prayed? Would you do it differently now? Why?

Let's pray together

"*Adonai* (ad-o-noy´), Lord, we are not patient. It's so hard to wait. And Lord, we are not always trusting. We are doers, and it's so very hard to trust that you are working when we can't see the end. Help us relinquish control and trust your goodness. Keep our eyes on Jesus, who has *kâlâh* (kaw-law) our redemption. We are forever indebted to you. Amen."

A Gate with Power

Ša'ar (shah'-ar)
RUTH 4:1–2

After our expedited wedding, Mike's unit was selected to deactivate rather than deploy. Working for the military is like that. Plans change all the time. Though thankful for this news, the chances for deployment still hung in the air like a threatening cloud on the horizon. We knew a phone call could change our future at any moment, and we knew a war could break out soon.

A month after we said, "I do," we started our family. I was thrilled, scared, and green. Morning sickness was renamed all-day sickness—the honeymoon hadn't lasted long. Real life moved in and unpacked its bags.

Months passed, the all-day sickness dissipated, and the threat of deployment waned. We seemed to be in a good place. A safe place. Until the phone call came a few days after Christmas. Mike's unit was reactivated and scheduled to go to war.

Mike boarded a plane for Iraq on January 14, 1991, leaving his pregnant newlywed wife and unborn child behind. I struggled with his excitement. But I soon realized soldiers train for this. This is why they serve. And looking back, this war proved a great one to fight in. The battle unbalanced. The advantage ours.

E-mail didn't exist at that time. Snail mail and phone calls were our only forms of communication, but my soldier served in a battalion with access to phones, unlike many soldiers. I went to sleep praying for a call to wake me in the middle of the night, and every other week it did.

The war ended quickly, and four months later and a week before Lamaze classes, Mike's unit was scheduled to return home. I didn't have to write the President of the United States to petition my husband's return for the birth of his first child. That was a relief. I didn't think the president would agree anyway.

On the night of their return, the time of the battalion's arrival continued to change. With each update I held my breath and my heart. I wouldn't allow joy or excitement until I saw Mike's face. Many friends joined me to welcome him on his return, but thinking back to that dark Texas night, I don't think either one of us allowed our hearts to be free until we walked through the front door of our little blue home on Pearl Street. For a moment we were strangers—both changed. Mike had witnessed war. I had gained fifty pounds with a baby doing cartwheels inside.

But the moment we walked across our threshold, the *šaʿar* to our house, we were newlyweds again. My husband was home.

Digging for treasure

1. Read Ruth 4:1. Where did Boaz go?

2. Who walked by?

3. Do you think Boaz knew the man would be walking by the city gates or do you think it was chance? Why?

4. Did the man have a name? Why would the author choose not to give him a name?

You've learned so much! I'm proud of you. You're exactly right; the man's name is irrelevant. But some commentators also believe the author didn't reveal his identity because he didn't accept his kinsman duties—he didn't deserve a name. We'll just call him "the nameless one." But in modern English Boaz yelled, "Hey, you! Yeah, you! Come over here and sit down."

But the nameless one was not the only one Boaz called to the gates.

5. Read Ruth 4:2. Who were the others invited to join the meeting? What did Boaz tell them to do?

6. Why would they obey Boaz?

There are some who believe Boaz was a judge.

7. He does seem to have authority. Did any of his prior actions reveal judge-like qualities?

He's familiar with the law and intent on following it.

Let's talk about the city gate for a moment and the role it played during this time. According to the *Archeological Study Bible*, the city gate, the *Ša'ar*, played an important role in the city's defense. If a group of people possessed the gate of the city, they controlled the city itself. But the gate also played an important role in the economic, legal, and civic affairs of the city. Here judges judged and elders decided civic matters. The gate signified status. "To sit in the city gate among the elders denoted honor, while the right to enter the city gate indicated citizenship."[1]

The city gate held great significance. It's seen throughout the Bible.

Connecting with other Scripture

8. Read Job 29:7–17. How did the young men and elders show their respect to Job? Where was he?

9. What did Job do for people when he was at the city gate?

10. Does this remind you of anyone? Explain.

The city gate was a place of judgment.

11. Read Deuteronomy 22:23. Where are the two people stoned?

12. Does the Deuteronomy passage remind you of any of the dangers one of our most beloved biblical characters faced with her pregnancy?

Despite the danger, Mary consented to God's plan.

13. Read Hebrews 13:12–14.

- Where did Jesus suffer?
- What are we looking for?

14. Read Revelation 21:1–7 and 22:14. What city gates will those who've been redeemed walk through?

Can you imagine what it's going to be like to walk through those gates? Close your eyes. Picture yourself walking through the gates of the New Jerusalem. What do you see or feel?

There's one more gate I want us to see.

15. Read John 10:7–11.

- What did Jesus claim to be?
- How did Jesus become the gate?

I'm mixing my metaphors, but I don't want us to miss the power and authority of the city gate or the sheep gate. Jesus died outside the city gates where people were judged on a daily basis. This was a moment of judgment as Boaz stood before the elders and witnesses. Boaz will provide Ruth and Naomi's redemption, but Jesus not only bought us with his life outside the city gates, he *became* the gate to enter into peace with God. As we walk through that gate, we will be citizens of the New Jerusalem. Ruth will soon have a new legal citizenship, too.

Bringing the treasure home to our hearts

Describe the day you chose to believe in Jesus, to enter the gate of heavenly citizenship.

Let's pray together

"*Adonay* (Ad-o-noy´), thank you for being a righteous, faithful, and loving God. Thank you for Jesus, who took our punishment outside the city gates so we can enter the heavenly *ša'ar* (shah´-ar) redeemed and citizens of your kingdom. Amen."

Truth Uncovered

Gâlâh (gaw-law')
RUTH 4:3–6

This December day perched on the calendar only a few squares away from Christmas and a few rows before my sixth birthday. I was one of those "blessed" children who often received Christmas and birthday gifts rolled into one because I arrived into the world only two weeks after Jesus was born. I really hated having a birthday so close to December 25, but there was nothing I could do about it.

I loved my Papaw. He was a wrinkly old cowboy who loved surprises. I spent a lot of time with him on his farm riding horses, helping herd cattle into pens, and racing the horses to the barn (only because the horses smelled the barn, and we were at their mercy). He let me drive his pickup all by myself as I followed his tractor—I was only twelve.

But on this day I wasn't at the farm, I was home as I peered out our kitchen window watching my beloved Papaw walk up our driveway. He was carrying a big cardboard box on his shoulder. I darted out the back door into the December chill to greet him with excited curiosity. My mom had told me he was bringing me an early birthday present—though we hadn't opened Christmas gifts yet.

"Whatcha got, Papaw?" I wailed.

"Just a sack of taters," he replied with a smirk.

As if on cue, my gift poked his fuzzy little puppy dog head into the air. My Papaw's secret was *gâlâh*—uncovered for all to see. A silver toy poodle awaited my arms. I named him Sparky, my best friend's dog's name. He fit perfectly in our Christmas stockings that year.

That was the best dual Christmas-birthday present ever. Maybe being born so close to Jesus' birth *was* a good thing.

Digging for treasure

1. Read Ruth 4:3. What did Boaz reveal to the nameless one, the kinsman-redeemer?

As we covered briefly on Day 1—when we started with the end rather than the beginning, it's likely that Naomi's husband, Elimelech, sold or leased their land to fund their move. God had provided laws regarding the buying and selling of his people's land.

2. Read Leviticus 25:23–28. Could land be sold permanently?

3. What was the responsibility of the kinsman-redeemer?

4. What could a man do if he did not have a kinsman-redeemer, but he acquired wealth sufficient to buy his land back?

5. What would happen to the land if the man did not have a kinsman or couldn't buy the land back?

Boaz tells the kinsman-redeemer, "Naomi, who has come back from the country of Moab, is *selling* the parcel of land that belonged to our relative Elimelech." (Ruth 4:3, emphasis added)

Wait a minute. Was the land Naomi's to sell? Did Naomi somehow get a message to Boaz that she wanted to sell it? There are questions that have no answers, so we must stick with what we do know according to what we just read. Always base your interpretation and understanding on the context of what the Bible does say. Whether or not Naomi's family leased or sold their land, the law provided for the means to reclaim it. If she didn't own it, it needed to be redeemed by a kinsman-redeemer. If she did own it, she certainly could not farm it herself. Because of the context of the story and the need for a redeemer, I concur with the *Archeological Study Bible* that Naomi was selling her right of redemption to a kinsman.[1]

6. Read Ruth 4:4. How does your Bible translate the first sentence of this verse?

The English Standard Version reads, "So I thought I would tell[1540] you of it and say, 'Buy it in the presence of those seated here and in the presence of the elders of my people."

7. Find **1540** in the Old Testament Dictionary in the back of this book. What is the Hebrew word, and when have we seen this word used?

We studied this word on Day 18. On that day, Ruth did the *uncovering*. Today, Boaz revealed what he could've left hidden.

8. What did Boaz suggest?

9. Do you think it was a good thing Naomi and Ruth weren't among the crowd at the city gate? Why? Would you be worried if you were Ruth?

ABSOLUTELY! If I were Ruth, it would've been a *really* good thing I was not there. Even if I appeared to maintain my composure, my heart would've been at the bottom of my stomach at this point in the meeting.

I wonder if this worried Boaz. But he was a man who follows the law.

10. What does Boaz tell the other kinsman about his rights?

11. What does Boaz tell him to do if he does not want to redeem the land?

12. What was the other kinsman's response?

Now, it's probably a *really* good thing Ruth was not there. She might have fainted or made a scene. Knowing me, I would've started crying, praying like crazy for God to do something.

But good ol' Boaz had an ace up his sleeve. He had yet to *galāh* one more important detail.

13. What was the catch to this *almost too good to be true* deal for the kinsman? (v. 5)

14. How does Boaz describe Ruth? Why do you think he chose to introduce her this way?

15. Why would the kinsman also acquire Ruth with this purchase?

Hold on . . . Boaz linked two laws into one. The first was the law concerning redeeming family property. The second was the levirate law that legally bound a man to marry his brother's widow if she bore no son to carry on his name. Mahlon's brother is dead. Legally, neither Boaz nor the nameless one was obligated to marry Ruth. But as Liz Higgs put it, "Buying the land is a legal obligation; marrying Ruth is a moral obligation."[2]

Did the *galah*, or uncovering, of Ruth change the kinsman's decision? Why? (v. 6)

I know everyone thinks less of the nameless one for his decision, but I'm really glad he chickened out, aren't you? He didn't want to endanger his family. He chose what was best for them, but Boaz did tell him that he (Boaz) would step up as redeemer if the nameless one wouldn't. I see this as a lesson in God's grace. It's okay to say "no."

I'm reminded that I don't always have to be the savior in a situation. If we don't have the freedom or grace to fulfill an obligation, we need to trust that God has someone else waiting to step up when we can't. But that's just a sidenote.

The main lesson is found in Boaz. Again, we can know Christ by watching Boaz carefully. Though he was just a man, and Ruth and Naomi very human women, their story *reveals* the heart of Jesus and God's plan of redemption for the Gentiles and his people, the Jews.

Boaz's law-abiding actions exemplify the lengths Jesus went to in order to redeem us according to spiritual laws beyond our comprehension. Before Jesus was crucified outside the city gates, he revealed that there was no other way for redemption to be accomplished. He followed the rules. He obeyed.

Connecting with other Scripture

16. Read Matthew 26:36–45. How many times did Jesus ask God to take "this cup" away from him? Did God release Jesus from following the plan?

Many commentators understand "this cup" to be symbolic of the wrath of God. But there is another "cup" I want us to see. I find it fascinating.

17. Read Matthew 26:19–30. What dinner did Jesus and the disciples share together?

Have you participated in a Passover meal, a *seder*? If you have not, I encourage you to do so. Every aspect of the meal points to Christ. It helps us understand why Christ broke the bread and passed the cup. Each cup represents God's promises to Israel; the order is very important. In fact, *seder* means "order."[3] These are the promises:

> "Say therefore to the people of Israel, 'I am the LORD, and I will bring
> you out from under the burdens of the Egyptians, and I will deliver you
> from slavery to them, and I will redeem you with an outstretched arm
> and with great acts of judgment. I will take you to be my people, and I
> will be your God, and you shall know that I am the LORD your God, who

has brought you out from under the burdens of the Egyptians'" (Exodus 6:6–7).

The four cups of the *seder:*

- First Cup: Cup of Sanctification
- Second Cup: Cup of Deliverance
- Third Cup: Cup of Redemption
- Fourth Cup: Cup of Completion

18. Read Matthew 26:27. How does Jesus describe this cup?

Theologians believe that this was the third cup—the Cup of Redemption.

19. Read Hebrews 9:19–28 and answer these questions:

- What does the law require for cleansing? (v. 22)
- Why will Christ not have to suffer again? (vv. 25–26)
- Why did Christ come the first time, and why will he come a second? (v. 28)

20. Flip back to Matthew 26:29. What did Jesus say about the last cup, or taking any more drinks during the dinner?

I find this fascinating. Jesus told the disciples, "I will not drink of the Cup of Completion until I drink it with you in *my Father's kingdom.*" Whether or not the disciples completed that meal, we do not know, but we know Jesus didn't. But one day he will.

There's one more thing I want us to see. Let's read the last half of Hebrews 9:28 that explains why Jesus is coming a second time: "... not to deal with sin but to save those who are <u>eagerly waiting</u>[553] for him." (Hebrews 9:28)

21. Locate **553** in the New Testament Dictionary in the back of this book. What word jumps out in this definition?

Apekdechomai (ap-ek-dekh'-om-ahee). Say that word three times fast. It's a great word that means so much more than "waiting." It means "waiting with great expectation." Christ came to die for man's sin the first time. But when he comes back the second time, he will come for *all* who are waiting for him with great expectation.

22. What other people group besides Christians is waiting for Messiah to come?

Yes. The Jews. His people are waiting for him to come. They are waiting his "first" arrival and we are waiting for his second. But we must never forget that they are God's people.

23. Read Romans 11:25-27. Will the Jews be saved when Jesus comes back?

24. Read Romans 11:28,29. What does Paul call the Jews as far as the "election" is concerned? Why?

So, both Christians and Jews are waiting. And so was Ruth. She was waiting to find out how the legal proceedings ended. Would she be redeemed by one she did not know or her beloved Boaz?

Bringing the treasure home to our hearts

Share a time when a secret or something simply not known to many was revealed. What happened? Was it good for this unknown thing to be known?

To whom do you relate the most in this part of the story: Boaz (doing what needs to be done), Ruth (waiting, unable to do anything), or the kinsman who declines his duties but knows someone else will fulfill them?

Let's pray together

Dear God, *gâlâh* (gaw-law') anything in our lives that keeps us from knowing you more fully. Open our eyes and hearts to your people, the Jews, and the meaning of everything you've commanded them to do. This will help us know you better. We wait expectantly for your return. Amen.

Redemption Duty

G^eullāh (geh-ool-law)

RUTH 4:6–8

She stared down the five-foot drop as if it were twenty. I realize that when you're only three feet tall, five feet is a long way down, but I stood right there. My momma arms were outstretched. I could catch any fall. Yet she whined, "I can't do it!"

I wasn't forcing my three-year-old to slide down the firepole from the fort at the top of the slide; this was her idea. She wanted to do it, but she couldn't take the leap. We stood in the hot Carolina sun—my patience melting. I needed a nap as badly as she did.

Then it happened. My patience not only melted but evaporated, and I commanded, "Lauren! Slide down the pole or I'm going to spank you!"

The whines immediately stopped. Like a toy soldier she snapped to attention, grabbed the pole and slid to the grass. "I wanna do it again!" she triumphantly shouted as she ran up the ladder.

I've thought back to that day many times and prayed for God to redeem it. Even though my baby girl pushed through her fear, I grieved over my threatening words that got her to the ground.

Twenty years after that traumatic moment my grown Lauren stood in the kitchen one afternoon talking about college graduation and describing her teaching internship. She explained, "Mom, it was a firepole moment. I just gritted my teeth and jumped."

She then proceeded to tell me how throughout the years that day in the park had become a catalyst to accomplish things she was afraid to do.

Redemption.

I was amazed and so thankful. My Jesus continues his *ge'ullāh*, his redemption duties for all my mistakes—even those bad mommy days. Praise him!

Digging for treasure

1. Read Ruth 4:6. We talked about this briefly yesterday, but why did the kinsman-redeemer change his mind?

"I cannot redeem it for myself, lest I <u>impair</u>[7843] my own inheritance . . ."

2. Look up **7843** and choose three words out of the definition that seem applicable to this context.

3. Are these definitions for *šāḥat* more threatening or powerful than the word "impair"?

Explain your thoughts.

4. Would you do something to help out someone else if it would possibly destroy or ruin your estate—your family's inheritance? Why?

Some commentators theorize that this man didn't want to redeem the land because he feared Ruth would bear many children who would cost him money to feed and clothe. Who knows? Maybe he had a jealous wife. Whatever the reason, aren't we relieved? I know Ruth would've been if she weren't sitting at home waiting. This was one rejection she was thankful for, I'm sure.

Rejection stings. Can you think of a time when you were thankful for a rejection? Did your relief come years later or immediately?

Let's keep digging. I hope you don't mind, but I'm taking you on a grammar rabbit trail for a brief moment. The kinsman continued his speech in verse 6: ". . . Take my right of redemption[1353] yourself for I cannot redeem[1350] it." The New International Version reads, "You redeem it yourself. I cannot do it."

After comparing other translations, the ESV got this one right in my book. Remember, it often takes more than one English word to translate the meaning of a Hebrew word, which is what happened in this case.

5. Locate **1353** in the Old Testament Dictionary in the back of this study. What part of speech is this word?

Write down what this part of speech does. (You may have to Google it or look in a dictionary if your eighth-grade grammar class is fuzzy.)

6. Find **1350** in the Old Testament Dictionary and list what part of speech it is.

Write these two Hebrew words side by side and notice the difference in spelling. Next to each word label its <u>part of speech.</u> What do these <u>parts of speech</u> have in common?

Perhaps I'm a bit obsessive when it comes to translation, but if there are two different Hebrew words written by ancient hands, I cannot translate them with the same English word even though they are very close in meaning. Though both Hebrew words are connected by the same verb, one of them is a participle—*gᵉ'ullāh* is a verb that acts like a noun.

Why is this important? I'm so glad you asked. We must never lose sight of the fact that only kinsmen in the family line could redeem. Joe Schmo off the streets couldn't buy the land and redeem Ruth to continue her husband's name—only someone who held the *duty of redemption* or *the right of redemption*—the *gᵉ'ullāh*.

This is paramount in our redemption into God's family, too. Only Jesus holds the *gᵉ'ullāh*. End of rabbit trail. Let's continue to dig.

7. Read Ruth 4:7. What was the custom of the day for the legal transaction?

8. What action could Ruth have taken if she stood between Boaz and the nameless kinsman-redeemer? Do you remember what a woman could do if the redeemer refused? (It had to do with a sandal.)

No spitting occurred this day. Probably a good thing.

9. Read Ruth 4:8. How did the kinsman-redeemer instruct Boaz, and what did the nameless man do?

10. What is Boaz buying?

There's another beautiful redemption story in the book of Jeremiah that involves buying land.

Connecting with other Scripture

11. Read Jeremiah 32:6–15. Who came to Jeremiah asking for help?

12. What did he want Jeremiah to do?

13. Why did Jeremiah agree to his cousin's plea even though he knew the Babylonians were going to take over the land? (vv. 6–7)

14. Where were they when the transaction was finalized? Were there witnesses?

15. What did Jeremiah instruct Baruch to do? Why?

16. Read Jeremiah 32:36–41. What does God promise?

I love the *Complete Jewish Bible*'s translation of these verses:

> "They will be my people, and I will be their God. I will give them sin-gleness of heart and singleness of purpose, so that they will fear me forever—this will be for their own good and for the good of their children after them. I will make with them an everlasting covenant not to turn away from them, but to do them good. I will plant them in this land truly, with my whole heart and being." (Jeremiah 32:38–41 CJB)

17. What speaks to you in these verses?

Come back with me to the story of Ruth for a minute to answer these questions:

18. To where did Naomi's family move?

19. Could the death of her husband and sons be part of God's plan?

20. Did God restore her land to her?

21. What do Naomi's story and God's actions in Jeremiah tell you about God's character and love?

22. Read Luke 15:11–31 and answer these questions:

* Who was more thankful? The son who came back or the one who never left?

* Was the father's reaction fair? Why?

* What does this story tell you about God's love?

This story tells me that we can't earn God's love; he's always waiting for us, and *all that he has* is ours (Luke 15:31).

Bringing the treasure home to our hearts

What does it mean to you that God keeps his promises even when we do not?

Let's pray together

"Dear God, thank you for your steady, unwavering faithfulness—your promises that never end. We are humbled by your love for us and willingness to do whatever it takes to *gâ'al* us. We also look eagerly for the day when your chosen people, the Jews, are also redeemed because you accepted your *geʾullāh* (*geh-ool-law*) so many years ago. Amen."

Never Severed

Kārat (kaw-rath)
RUTH 4:9–10

Even as a young girl I loved giving speeches.

But I often feel like Moses, slow of speech and tongue—I don't possess the best speaking voice or diction. My Oklahoma accent sounds more like a speech impediment at times, and I've wondered if it is one, but when I go back home I realize I'm just talking like the sweet people who raised me.

Despite my less than perfect voice, I love to speak to twenty-five or twenty-five hundred.

I entered every 4-H speech and demonstration contest I could. Most people assume 4-H participation involves raising and showing animals. But I was not one of those girls. I did bake and sew, but giving speeches ranked as my favorite contest.

That love for speaking grew as I entered high school and joined the Forensics Club. No, it wasn't a science club, but a speaking one. Big paper tongues hung on our lockers marking our membership.

I participated in many competitions, but only one stands out in my mind. I recited a poem by Robert Frost entitled "Out, Out." To this day I'm not sure what possessed me to perform this haunting poem except it was just that—haunting. I could practice my love for drama as my voice rose to crescendos and fell to soft whispers.

"Out, Out" was based on a tragic true story of Frost's neighbor whose young son died after a chain saw accident. The boy's hand was *kārat*, completely severed. I shiver even as I write those words. Forgive me for relating this gruesome story. This was the best example to define the Hebrew word. When something is *kārat* it is cut off. It can never be restored, just as the young boy's hand and his life could not.

I don't recall how the judges scored my speech, but I do remember their faces. They looked much like yours probably does right now.

Digging for treasure

1. Read Ruth 4:9–10. Boaz announced his purchase of Naomi's property and his acquisition of Ruth. What reason does he give for marrying Ruth?

"Also Ruth the Moabite, the widow of Mahlon, I have bought to be my wife, to perpetuate the name of the dead in his inheritance, that the name of the dead will not be <u>cut off</u>[3772] from among his brothers . . ."

2. Read the definition for **3772** in the Old Testament Dictionary in the back of this book. What are the two separate meanings of this word?

Context of the verse always reveals the meaning. Though *kārat* can refer to "cutting a covenant," in this context the word refers to something being eliminated or "cut off."

3. What is the significance of the meaning of this word in this context?

If something is cut off it can never be put back. Think of cutting off a branch from a tree. If something disappears, you might find it—as the New International Version chooses to translate this Hebrew word. But *kārat* ushers finality into its meaning.

Boaz married Ruth so Mahlon (or his name) would never be cut off from the family or town records. This is *chêsêd*. Though I think Boaz was going to benefit from having Ruth as a wife, he explained to the crowd that he was doing this for Mahlon. This *chêsêd* cannot be returned.

4. Ruth wasn't standing there, but do you think this reason would please her or upset her? How would you feel about Boaz's reasoning?

We read Scripture with our biases, through our filters. If you believe Ruth loved Mahlon—a belief probably resulting from your own good marriage or relationships, you probably believed that Boaz's reasons blessed Ruth. If you've been in a bad marriage, you might perceive Ruth's feelings differently. Am I right? Always keep this in mind when you study Scripture.

Has someone whose name you wanted to keep alive died too soon? What did you do to perpetuate their name and memory?

5. What does Boaz call the people listening to his proclamation?

6. Why are witnesses important?

7. If witnesses are important, would Ruth's proposal to Boaz, or his acceptance, while they were alone on the threshing floor, have been valid?

No. Boaz is not only a rule follower, he is a wise man. They needed witnesses to make the decision final. Notice that the witnesses here are more important than having Ruth or Naomi present.

Connecting with other Scripture

8. Read Deuteronomy 19:15. Could one witness's testimony make a judgment or settle a matter? How many were needed?

9. Read Acts 1:8. What does Jesus tell his followers?

10. Look up *martus,* **3144** in the New Testament Dictionary in the back of this book. Give a brief synopsis of the definition.

11. Why are witnesses (*martus*) important?

12. Read Acts 1:9–11. How did Christ leave the earth?

13. What did the men in white robes tell the disciples?

14. Read Revelation 1:5. What is Jesus called?

15. What was Christ the witness to?

16. Read Revelation 1:4–7. This is such a powerful Scripture passage. The blood pumping through Boaz's veins gave him the right to redeem Naomi's land and Ruth. But these verses tell us what Christ's blood did:

- What have we been made through Christ's love and blood?

- How is he coming back?

- Who will witness his arrival?

Can you imagine? Every time I see beautiful puffy clouds outlined by the sun or rays escaping through vaporous holes, I get excited. The clouds are a promise to me. Maybe Jesus will come on a gray, cloudy day. Just maybe. Perhaps this will help us endure less-than-sunny days. He's coming in the clouds.

I've been thinking about how a kinsman-redeemer carried on the name of the dead. Their name was not removed from the city ledgers (Ruth 4:10). Our names are so important to us—they were even more so in biblical days, but our names will be important in the future, too.

17. Read Revelation 20:15. What will happen to those whose name is not written in the Book of Life?

We cannot earn our redemption just as Naomi and Ruth couldn't earn theirs. Not only did they not have the funds to redeem the land, they did not have the family blood. Marriage bound them to Elimelech's family, not blood. That's why they needed a kinsman-redeemer.

We too need a redeemer. A *Gâa'l*. Not only did the blood in Jesus' veins bind him to this redemption duty, he purchased us *with* that precious blood—his own blood.

Bringing the treasure home to our hearts

Do you have any doubt that your name is written in the Book of Life? If you do, there's no time like the present to take care of that. Simply write a prayer asking Jesus to redeem you and thank him for redeeming you. If you know Jesus is your Redeemer, write him a prayer of thanksgiving implementing all we've learned in this lesson:

* We won't be cut off.
* Our names are in the book.

Let's pray together

"Jesus, thank you for being our kinsman-redeemer, our big "G" *Gâa'l* (Gaw-al). We will never be *kārat* (kaw-rath) from God's family because our name is written in your Book of Life. How do we thank you? How do we praise you? Make us loud witnesses of your love and the saving power of your blood. Amen."

Day 30

Seeds Planted for Generations

Zera (zeh´-rah)

RUTH 4:11–12

I want to have a green thumb when I grow up.

Almost fifty, I still aspire to be like my mom in this way. Her plants were always beautiful and thriving. Today mine don't look happy—more like creation groaning for Jesus to come back. They need attention.

I've worked on my green thumb for years, and in my journey to grow healthy, happy plants, I've learned some important precepts along the way. A huge lesson I discovered is that plants need food as well as water. When I fertilize my plants, they are greener and grow fuller.

One day as I fertilized my geraniums, this thought danced through my mind: *Prayer is like water, and reading the Bible is like food. You need **both** to grow spiritually healthy.*

This thought went straight from my head to my heart because it's easy for me to pray all day, but I must be intentional when I read my Bible. It requires effort.

I confess that during the winter months I don't take care of my indoor plants or the outdoor ones as I should. I get lazy. I forget. Sometimes they don't get water, much less food. They limp through to the spring.

I do the same in my spiritual life, too. Some seasons I consistently study, read, and pray, watering and feeding my soul. But other seasons I become too busy or lazy, and my spirit begins to wither. My leaves began to fade, and the spiritual *zera*—the seeds planted in me—cannot grow to bear fruit.

Digging for treasure

1. Read Ruth 4:11. What was the blessing the elders gave Boaz concerning Ruth?

2. Do you know the story of Rachel and Leah? I'll give a quick summary. (To read the whole story, go to Genesis 29:16–35 and 30:1–22.) Rachel and Leah were sisters. Jacob loved Rachel but was tricked into marrying Leah. Leah was blessed with children, but Rachel was barren.

Read Genesis 30:22–24. What happened?

3. What does Ruth have in common with Rachel? (Ruth 4:13)

It must be noted that Rachel and Leah, and their maidservants who gave birth to children when the two sisters could not, produced the sons who became the twelve tribes of Israel.

4. What was the second part of the blessing concerning Boaz? (v. 11)

Important words lie in this blessing. "May you act[6213] worthily[2428] in Ephrathah and be renowned in Bethlehem . . ."

5. Locate **6213** in the Old Testament Dictionary in the back of this book and write down the word you would've chosen to translate 'âśâh.

6. Look up **2428** in the Old Testament Dictionary. When have we studied this word before? What does *chayil* mean? What <u>part of speech</u> is it?

7. Now that you know the Hebrew counterparts, how would you translate this blessing conferred upon Boaz?

"This word has the basic idea of strength and influence." (CWSDOT)

The blessing was for Boaz to achieve *chayil,* which in this context fits the definitions of *power* and *influence.*

8. Read Ruth 4:12. To whom do the elders compare Ruth and Boaz in their blessing?

This is another painful story in the Bible. It's found in Genesis 38. Tamar's story is one of *levirate* law. She was married to Judah's sons. Both were wicked, and the Lord

put both to death. Judah did not uphold his promise to Tamar to give her his young-
est son, so she tricked Judah by posing as a prostitute. She conceived and revealed
the truth to Judah, who acknowledged his sin. Tamar gave birth to twins, Perez and
Zerah.

9. What was the exact blessing in verse 12?

> ". . . and may your house be like the house of Perez whom Tamar bore
> to Judah, because of the <u>offspring</u>[2233] that the Lord will give you by this
> woman." (Ruth 4:12)

If we skip over the whole sleeping-with-your-father-in-law thing, Tamar carried on
the name of Judah through the sons she bore. And Judah's tribe numbered 76,500
(Numbers 26:22). That's a BIG family!

10. Find **2233** in the Old Testament Dictionary. What is the Hebrew word, and what
does it mean?

Can you visualize the blessing of the *seed* planted that would bless for generations to
come? That seed was carefully, lovingly planted (*nāthan*) inside Ruth's womb as we
learned in our very first lesson.

But the Bible speaks of an imperishable seed planted within us, too.

Connecting with other Scripture

11. Read 1 Peter 1:22–25. Answer the following questions:

- What kind of seed (perishable or imperishable) lives in those who are born
  again?

- Through what are we born? What (or who) has given us this everlasting life?

- What is the everlasting seed that lives and breathes in us?

12. Read Matthew 13:18–23. Answer the following questions:

- What represents the seed sown along the path?

- What happens to the one whose roots aren't deep and what causes this?

- What are the thorns that choke out the word?

- The good soil represents whom?

13. Why would Jesus use the imagery of planting seeds?

I have a dear friend who worries that her soil is not good. She fears that she will be the one whose seed is choked out. But Jesus is very clear about the way we can have good soil. He says, ". . . this is the one who hears the word and understands it." (v. 23)

He also reveals what can choke out the word in our lives: ". . . the cares of this world and the deceitfulness of riches." (v. 22)

Bringing the treasure home to our hearts

Have you feared that the Word of God, the seed planted in you, will not survive? If so, write a prayer asking God to open your mind to his Word, to help you understand it. He is faithful. Also pray to trust Jesus in every aspect in your life—even when things are bad. Give God your cares, and pray to be content with what you have. End your prayer with thanks for three (or more) things in your life. The seed can grow when it's watered with thankfulness and fertilized with trust in God's goodness.

Let's pray together

"Jesus, we praise you! Thank you for the *zera* (zeh´-rah) planted inside us by your hand. Lord, help us understand your Word. Grow our roots deep as we trust you— help us trust you. Please make our lives fruitful. May many be born into the family of God as we plant seeds sharing your truth. Amen."

A Little Boy Named "Worshipper"

Ebed (eh´bed)

RUTH 4:14–22

When I was in college, the tiny Methodist Church where I served as the youth minister held a revival. The speakers were two talented women who not only taught about the importance of 24/7 worship but also sang and played instruments leading the handful of congregants in praise. I hadn't seen or heard anything like it; they raised their hands! These ladies talked about praising and worshipping God even on the bad days when you didn't feel like it. They taught us to sing and worship while washing dishes and changing dirty diapers, mowing the lawn and changing flat tires.

A few years later, after marriage and children, these precepts were my salvation. Being a stay-at-home mom was not easy. I missed working. But I intentionally worshipped God throughout the day, dirty dishes, dirty diapers, temper tantrums (including mine), and sleepless nights. It wasn't easy, but the presence of the Holy Spirit often filled me and gave me joy despite the spit-up on my shirt and the bags under my eyes. What's even more important, my children grew up watching me live that way—worshipping throughout the day, and they now are worshippers, too.

I want nothing more than to be an *ebed* of God. A servant. A slave. A worshipper.

Digging for treasure

1. Read Ruth 4:13. How was the elder's blessing for children fulfilled?

2. Read Ruth 4:14–15. What do the women proclaim about the kinsman-redeemer? How does your Bible translate this? (v. 15a)

Oh, friends, we found a treasure.

* "He shall be to you a <u>restorer</u>[7725] of life and a nourisher of your old age." (ESV)

* "He will <u>renew</u> your life and sustain you in your old age." (NIV)

I was so surprised to learn the Hebrew counterpart for *restorer* or *renew*.

3. Find the Hebrew word for **7725** in the Old Testament Dictionary in the back of this study and write it down as well as a couple of its definitions. Why would this excite me? When did we see this word earlier in the book?

Do you remember this word in the very beginning of our study? It's the same word Naomi used to command Orpah and Ruth to return to Moab (Ruth 1:11). Literally translated, the women prophesied, "He will *turn around* your life."

4. Who is turning around or returning Naomi's life? Is it Naomi or someone else?

Please don't miss this part. The <u>kinsman-redeemer</u> will turn her life around or return her life or renew her life . . . she cannot.

Have you tried to turn your life around? Were you strong enough? Did you need help?

5. Read the second half of the sentence in Ruth 4:15 regarding Naomi's daughter-in-law. What does it say?

Do you see the significance of this proclamation? OMG(osh)! This is huge, girl-friends. Men were revered in that culture. Sons were everything. But these ladies proclaim that Naomi's <u>daughter-in-law</u> is better than *seven* sons! Seven is not only a lot of boys, but it's a significant number in the Jewish culture, signifying completion or perfection.

So much is redeemed in this book. Even women. Do you see it? Do you agree? Share your thoughts.

6. Read Ruth 4:16–17. What did they name the baby?

I have fallen in love with the book of Ruth. There are so many powerful truths about our God and his faithfulness to redeem our broken lives. But this baby's name is the icing on the cake for me. Remember, names held purpose and meaning in biblical days. They were the essence of the person—prophetic of who he or she would become. Look at the meaning of their son's name:

'Ôb̄ed : "servant [worshipper]"[1]

7. What is the significance of *'Ôb̄ed's* name to you?

All was restored, redeemed. Naomi was redeemed back into her family but also back into her faith. She never seemed to stop believing in God, but her family's move did reveal a lack of trust in God's provision, and a belief they could handle the situation on their own. Maybe Elimelech was mad at God. The reason for their move to the profane country of Moab is not clear (besides the famine), but it is clear that Moab wasn't a good place for them to be. Other gods were worshiped in Moab.

Ruth, a foreigner, was also redeemed. She loved Naomi; supported her grieving mother-in-law, and vowed never to leave. She also vowed, "Your God will be my God." Her actions were *chêsêd* with hands and feet. Ruth left the gates of Moab as a worshipper of other gods, but she entered the gates of Bethlehem as a servant and worshipper of the one true God—the Jewish *'Elohiym.*

And Boaz, well, he always worshipped and served *'Elohiym, YHWH, Adonai.* He lived his faith right down to the last letter of the Law and goodness of his heart. God used this humble servant in a big way. And blessed him with a son.

8. What famous king is born in the line of *'Ôb̄ed* ? (Ruth 4:17)

9. Who is born out of the line of David? (Look back to our Day 1 lesson if you need a refresher.)

I wrote this on Day 1, but I feel it needs to be repeated here at the end:

What a family tree! Who would have thought that everyday, normal people, even unholy ones, would be the ancestors of Jesus? But they were. And two of those ancestors are the main characters of the book of Ruth. Two, unlikely, ordinary people living their lives, doing the best they could through drought and famine, heartache and grief. Common people used by God in a big way. It just goes to show . . . you never know what God is going to do.

But I will add—God uses people who worship him.

Connecting with other Scripture

10. Read Luke 1:38. How did Mary respond to Gabriel?

Doule' is a Greek word (remember the ancient New Testament manuscripts were written in Greek.) It means slave, or servant.

But Mary spoke Hebrew or Aramaic rather than Greek, and the Hebrew counterpart for *doule'* is *ebed*. In the Old Testament this Hebrew term was spoken in reference to slaves and submission to God, but it was also used in the context of one who *worshipped* YHWH.

11. When Mary called herself an *ebed* of the Lord, what was she proclaiming?

12. One more time, what does *'Ōḇēḏ* mean?

Do you see the similarities in these words? Both *'Ōbēd* and *ebed* come from the root word *abad,* a Hebrew verb that means to work or serve.

It's beautiful, isn't it? As Mary knelt down before Gabriel accepting her assignment, her words threaded back through generations to the birth of Ruth and Boaz's son—the one they named "servant" or "worshipper" of God. *'Ōbēd* would become the grandfather of David.

13. Read Acts 13:22. How does God describe David?

David was a worshipper. His psalms are testament to that.

14. What does God say David will do in Acts 13:22?

David was a servant of God.

15. Read Philippians 2:5–11. What was Christ's attitude? What did he make himself?

16. At what name will every knee bow?

17. What name will every tongue confess?

Oh . . . what a day of worship that will be!

Bringing the treasure home to our hearts

Are you an *ebed* of God? What does that look like in your life?

Now that you have studied the book of Ruth, what aspect of the many things we studied spoke deepest in your soul?

Let's pray together

"*Adonai* (Ad-o-noy´), we give you praise! Great and mighty things you have done. Make us as faithful as Boaz and Ruth. Make us *ebeds* (eh´beds), worshipping servants of the Most High. Thank you for Jesus, our *Gâa'l* (gaw-al). Thank you that we are redeemed forever. Let us be people of *chesed* (kheh´-sed), paying forward the *chesed* (kheh´-sed) you gave us in Jesus. We pray for your people, our Jewish friends. Draw them to you. Thank you for the promise of their redemption one day. Until then, help us love them. Amen."

    . . . How do I say goodbye? (I don't.)

You've run a marathon, my friends. Thank you for running with me. I'm so proud of you. I pray your cloak six measures full—three for you and three to give away. I can't wait to meet you in heaven one day. Until then, you can find me at: www.wordsbyandylee.com. Keep studying. Keep digging. The Lord be with you!

Redeemed,
andy

ENDNOTES

Day 1

1. Kaiser and Garrett, *Archeological Study Bible*, 393.

Day 2

1. Ruth 1:1, "Bethlehem" http://www.mystudybible.com
2. Zodhiates, Micah 5:2, *Key Word Study Bible*, 1085.
3. Berlin and Brettler, eds., *The Jewish Study Bible*, 1580.
4. Zodhiates, "Elimelech," 1906.
5. *Life Application Bible*, 391.
6. Hoerth, Mattingly and Edwin M. Yamauchi, eds., *People of the Old Testament World*, 330.

Day 3

1. Zodhiates, "'Orpāh," 1995.
2. Berlin and Brettler, eds., 1580.
3. Zodhiates, "Rûṯ," 2012.
4. *Quest Study Bible*, 369.
5. Ferguson, *Faithful God*, 25.

Day 4

1. Zodhiates, "Eleos," 1619.

Day 5

1. Ibid., "Mar," 1529.
2. Ibid., "Nâshaq," 1536.

Day 6

1. Spangler, *Praying the Names*, 15.
2. Curtis and Eldridge, *Sacred Romance*, 52–53.

3. Spangler, 74.

4. Zodhiates, John 1:1–17, 1238.

Day 7

1. John 10:10, "Perissós," http://www.mystudybible.com

Day 9

1. Brown, Fausett, and Jamieson, *Bethany Parallel Commentaries,* 498.

2. Zodhiates, 1129.

Day 10

1. Berlin and Brettler, 1581.

2. Zodhiates, "No<u>k</u>riy," 1534.

Day 11

1. Ibid., "Châsâh," 1517.

2. Ibid., "Pach," 1543.

Day 12

1. Ibid., "Lêb," 1524.

Day 13

1. Ibid., "Nā<u>k</u>ar," 1534.

Day 14

1. Ibid., "Chêsêd," 1516.

2. Ibid., "Āza<u>b</u>," 1538.

Day 15

1. Kaiser and Garrett, 186.

2. Zodhiates, "Tôb," 1519.

Day 16

1. "Hebrew Lexicon: H3190 (KJV)." Blue Letter Bible. Accessed 27 Oct 2014. http://www
.blueletterbible.org/lang/lexicon/lexicon.cfm?Strongs=H3190&t=KJV.

Day 17

1. Kula, *Yearnings,* 18.

2. Zodhiates, "Yâda," 1520.

Day 18

1. Ruth 3:11, "Margÿlot," https://bible.org/netbible

2. Deffinbaugh, Bob. "Cutting Corners: Naomi's Undercover Operation," *Ruth: A Story of Redemption—A Study of the Book of Ruth*, Copyright ©1996–2006 Bible.org, reprinted with permissions.

Day 20

1. Brown, Fausett, and Jamieson, 500.

2. "Hebrew Lexicon :: H3943 (KJV)." Blue Letter Bible. Accessed 27 Oct, 2014. http://www.blueletterbible.org/lang/lexicon/lexicon.cfm?Strongs=H3943&t=KJV

Day 21

1. Higgs, *The Girl's Still Got It*, 121.

2. Ibid., 123.

3. Ibid., 122.

Day 23

1. Zodhiates, "Chay," 1515.

Day 24

1. Daniel, Ron, "Study Notes: Ruth 3:1–4:10," http://rondaniel.com/library/08-Ruth/Ruth0301.html

2. Levin, Rabbi Dr. Meir. "Ruth: Boaz and Naomi," http://www.torah.org/learning/ruth/class32.html. reprinted with permission from Project Genesis-Torah.org

Day 25

1. Zodhiates, "Nāpal," 1534.

2. Ibid., "Kālāh," 1523.

3. Ibid., "Yasar," 1522.

4. Ibid., "'Ôrach," 1505.

Day 26

1. Kaiser and Garrett, 392.

Day 27

1. Ibid., 393.

2. Higgs, 147.

Day 31

1. Zodhiates, "'Ôḇēḏ," 1988.

BIBLIOGRAPHY

Baker, Warren P., and Spiros Zodhiates, eds. *Hebrew Greek Key Word Study Bible: English Standard Version*. Chattanooga: AMG Publishers, 2013.

Baker, Warren P., Eugene Carpenter, and Spiros Zodhiates. *The Complete Word Study Dictionary* (Combined Old and New Testament edition). Chattanooga: AMG Publishers, 2003. E-Sword iPad edition.

Berlin, Adele and Marc Zvi Brettler, eds. *The Jewish Study Bible*. New York: Oxford University Press, 2004.

Brown, Fausset, Jamieson, Clarke, and Henry. *The Bethany Parallel Commentaries on the Old Testament*. Minneapolis: Bethany House Publishers, 1985.

Curtis, Brent and John Eldridge. *The Sacred Romance: Drawing Closer to the Heart of God*. Nashville: Thomas Nelson, 1997.

Ferguson, Sinclair B. *Faithful God: An Exposition of the Book of Ruth*. Bridgend, UK: Bryntirion, 2005.

Higgs, Liz. *The Girl's Still Got It: Take a Walk with Ruth and the God Who Rocked Her World*. New York: WaterBrook Press, 2012.

Hoerth, Alfred J., Gerald L. Mattingly and Edwin M. Yamauchi, eds., *People of the Old Testament World*. Grand Rapids: Baker, 1998.

Life Application Bible: The Living Bible. Wheaton, Illinois: Tyndale House Publishers, Inc. and Youth for Christ/USA, 1988.

Kaiser, Walter C. Jr. and Duane A. Garrett, eds., *NIV Archeological Study Bible: An Illustrated Walk through Biblical History and Culture*. Grand Rapids: Zondervan, 2005.

Kula, Rabbi Irwin. *Yearnings: Embracing the Sacred Messiness of Life*. New York: Hyperion Publishers, 2006.

NET Bible. (www.bible.org): Bible Studies Press, 2005.

Quest Study Bible. Grand Rapids: Zondervan, 2003.

Spangler, Ann. *Praying the Names of God: A Daily Guide.* Grand Rapids: Zondervan, 2004.

Stern, David H. *The Complete Jewish Bible.* Clarksville, MD: Jewish New Testament Publications, Inc., 1998.

Zodhiates, Spiros, Th.D., ex. ed., *Hebrew-Greek Key Word Study Bible NIV.* Chattanooga, TN: AMG Publishers, 1996.

OLD TESTAMENT DICTIONARY

**Taken from
AMG's Annotated
Strong's Hebrew Dictionary
Of the Old Testament**

Additional materials in this dictionary were taken from
The Complete Word Study Dictionary: Old Testament
by Warren Baker and Eugene Carpenter.
©2003 by AMG Publishers. All Rights Reserved.

Transliteration of Hebrew Consonants

Hebrew Consonant	Name	Trans–literation	Phonetic Sound	Example
א	Aleph	ʾ	Silent	Similar to h in honor
ב	Beth	b	b	as in boy
ב	Veth	b	v	as in vat
ג	Gimel	g	g	as in get
ג	Gimel	g	g	as in get
ד	Daleth	d	d	as in do
ד	Daleth	d	d	as in do
ה	Hē	h	h	as in hat
ו	Waw	v	w	as in wait
ז	Zayin	z	z	as in zip
ח	Cheth	ch	ch	Similar to ch in the German ach
ט	Teth	ṭ	t	as in time
י	Yodh	y	y	as in you
כ	Kaph	k	k	as in kit
כ	Chaph	k	ch	Similar to ch in the German ach
ל	Lamed	*l*	l	as in lit
מ	Mem	m	m	as in move
נ	Nun	n	n	as in not
ס	Samekh	s	s	as in see
ע	Ayin	ʿ	Silent	Similar to h in honor
פ	Pē	p	p	as in put
פ	Phē	ph	f	as in phone
צ	Tsadde	ts	ts	as in wits
ק	Qoph	q	q	as in Qatar
ר	Resh	r	r	as in run
שׂ	Sin	ś	s	as in see
שׁ	Shin	sh	sh	as in ship
ת	Taw	t	t	as in time
ת	Thaw	th	th	as in this

Transliteration of Hebrew Vowels

Hebrew Vowel	Name	Position	Trans-literation	Sound
	Shewa (Silent)	מְ	*Not transliterated or pronounced*	
	Shewa (Vocal)	מְ	e	u as in but
	Pathah	מַ	a	a as in lad
	Hateph Pathah	מֲ	ă	a as in lad
	Qamets	מָ	â	a as in car
	Hateph Qamets	מֳ	ŏ	a as in car
	Sere Yodh	מֵי	êy	ey as in prey
	Sere	מֵ	ê	ey as in prey
	Seghol	מֶ	e	e as in set
	Hateph Seghol	מֱ	ĕ	e as in set
	Hiriq Yodh	מִי	îy	i as in machine
	Hiriq	מִ	i	i as in pin
	Qamets Qatan	מָ	o	o as in hop
	Holem	מֹ	ô	o as in go
ֹ	Holem	מוֹ	ôw	o as in go
	Qubbuts	מֻ	u	u as in put
ֹ	Shureq	מוּ	û	u as in tune

Special Symbols

:— (colon and one-em dash) are used within each entry to mark the end of the discussion of syntax and meaning of the word under consideration, and to mark the beginning of the list of word(s) used to render it in translation.

() (parentheses) denote, in the translation renderings only, a word or syllable given in connection with the principal word it follows.

+ (addition symbol) denotes a rendering in translation of one or more Hebrew words in connection with the one under consideration.

× (multiplication symbol) denotes a rendering within translation that results from an idiom peculiar to the Hebrew.

א (Aleph)
OT Numbers 1–871

410. אֵל, **'êl,** *ale*; shortened from 352; *strength*; as adjective *mighty*; especially the *Almighty* (but used also of any *deity*):—God (god), × goodly, × great, idol, might (-y one), power, strong. Compare names in "-el."

A masculine noun meaning God, god, mighty one, hero. This is one of the most ancient terms for God, god, or deity. It appears most often in Genesis, Job, Psalms, and Isaiah and not at all in some books. The root meaning of the word mighty can be seen in Job 41:25[17] and Mic 2:1. This word is used occasionally of other gods (Ex 34:14; Dt 3:24; Ps 44:20[21]; Mal 2:11) but is most often used to mean the one true God (Ps 5:4[5]; Isa 40:18). It expresses various ideas of deity according to its context. The most common may be noted briefly: the holy God as contrasted to humans (Hos 11:9); the High God El (Ge 14:18; 16:13; Eze 28:2); the Lord (Yahweh) as a title of Israel according to the Lord's own claim (Ge 33:20; Isa 40:18); God or god in general (Ex 34:14; Dt 32:21; Mic 7:8); the God of Israel, the Lord (Nu 23:8; Ps 118:27); God (Job 5:8).

This word is used with various descriptive adjectives or attributes: 'êl is God of gods (Ps 50:1); God of Bethel (Ge 35:7); a forgiving God (Ps 99:8). He is the holy God (Isa 5:16). Especially significant are the assertions declaring that 'êl is with us, Immanuel (Isa 7:14); and He is the God of our salvation (Isa 12:2); a gracious God (Ne 9:31); a jealous God (Ex 20:5; 34:14). The closeness of this God is expressed in the hand of God (Job 27:11).

In the human realm, the word also designates men of power or high rank (Eze 31:11); mighty men (Job 41:25[17]); or mighty warriors (Eze 32:21). The word is used to designate superior and mighty things in nature, such as mighty or high mountains (Ps 36:6[7]), lofty, high cedars, or stars (Ps 80:10[11]; Isa 14:13).

In conjunction with other descriptive words, it occurs as 'êl shaday, "God Almighty" (7706) (Ge 17:1; 28:3; Ex 6:3) or 'êl 'elyôwn, "God Most High" (5945) (Ge 14:18, 19; Ps 78:35). Used with hand (yâd) in some settings, the word conveys power, strength (Ge 31:29; Dt 28:32; Pr 3:27), or ability.

430. אֱלֹהִים, **'ĕlôhîym,** *el-o-heem'*; plural of 433; *gods* in the ordinary sense; but specifically used (in the plural thus, especially with the article) of the supreme *God*; occasionally applied by way of deference to *magistrates*; and sometimes as a superlative:—angels, × exceeding, God (gods) (-dess, -ly), × (very) great, judges, × mighty.

A masculine plural noun meaning God, gods, judges, angels. Occurring more than 2,600 times in the OT, this word commonly designates the one true God (Ge 1:1) and is often paired with God's unique name *yĕ hôwâh* (3068) (Ge 2:4; Ps 100:3). When the word is used as the generic designation of God, it conveys in Scripture that God is the Creator (Ge 5:1); the King (Ps 47:7[8]); the Judge (Ps 50:6); the Lord (Ps 86:12); and the Savior (Hos 13:4). His character is compassionate (Dt 4:31); gracious (Ps 116:5); and faithful to His covenant (Dt 7:9). In fewer instances, this word refers to foreign gods, such as Dagon (1Sa 5:7) or Baal (1Ki 18:24). It also might refer to judges (Ex 22:8[7], 9[8]) or angels as gods (Ps 97:7). Although the form of this word is plural, it is frequently used as if it were singular—that is, with a singular verb (Ge 1:1–31; Ex 2:24). The plural form of this word may be regarded (1) as intensive to indicate God's fullness of power; (2) as majestic to indicate God's kingly rule; or (3) as an allusion to the Trinity (Ge 1:26). The singular form of this word *'ĕ lôwah* (433) occurs only in poetry (Ps 50:22; Isa 44:8). The shortened form of the word is *'êl* (410).

734. אֹרַח, **'ôrach,** *o'-rakh*; from 732; a well trodden *road* (literal or figurative); also a *caravan*:—manner, path, race, rank, traveller, troop, [by-, high-] way.

A masculine noun meaning path, way, byway, or highway. It describes the literal path one walks on (Jgs 5:6); the path or rank one walks in (Joel 2:7). Figuratively, this word describes the path of an individual or course of life (Job 6:18); the characteristics of a lifestyle, good or evil (Ps 16:11); righteousness or judgment (Pr 2:13). It is further used to mean traveler or wayfarer (Job 31:32). In the plural, it means caravans or troops (Job 6:19).

ב (Beth)
OT Numbers 872–1340

1288. בָּרַךְ, **bârak,** *baw-rak'*; a primitive root; to *kneel*; (by implication) to *bless* God (as an act of adoration), and (vice-versa) man (as a benefit); also (by euphemism) to *curse* (God or the king, as treason):— × abundantly, × altogether, × at all, blaspheme, bless, congratulate, curse, × greatly, × indeed, kneel (down), praise, salute, × still, thank.

A verb meaning to bless, kneel, salute, or greet. The verb derives from the noun knee and perhaps suggests the bending of the knee in blessing. Its derived meaning is to bless someone or something. The verb is used when blessing God (Ge 9:26) or people (Nu 24:9). God used this verb when He blessed Abraham in the Abrahamic covenant (Ge 12:3). The word is used intensively when God blesses people or people bless each other (Jos 17:14). When the word is used reflexively, it describes a person blessing or congratulating himself (Dt 29:19 [20]). Other meanings are to bend the knee (2Ch 6:13); and to greet someone with a salutation or friendliness (1Sa 25:14).

ג (Gimel)
OT Numbers 1341–1667

1350. גָּאַל, **gâ'al,** *gaw-al´*; a primitive root, to *redeem* (according to the Oriental law of kinship), i.e. to *be the next of kin* (and as such to *buy back* a relative's property, *marry* his widow, etc.):— × in any wise, × at all, avenger, deliver, (do, perform the part of near, next) kinsfolk (-man), purchase, ransom, redeem (-er), revenger.

A verb meaning to redeem or act as a kinsman-redeemer. The word means to act as a redeemer for a deceased kinsman (Ru 3:13); to redeem or buy back from bondage (Le 25:48); to redeem or buy back a kinsman's possessions (Le 25:26); to avenge a kinsman's murder (Nu 35:19); to redeem an object through a payment (Le 27:13). Theologically, this word is used to convey God's redemption of individuals from spiritual death and His redemption of the nation of Israel from Egyptian bondage and also from exile (see Ex 6:6).

1353. גְּאֻלָּה, **gᵉullâh,** *geh-ool-law´*; feminine passive participle of 1350; *redemption* (including the right and the object); by implication *relationship*:—kindred, redeem, redemption, right.

A feminine singular noun meaning redemption. The term is typically used in legal texts denoting who can redeem (Le 25:24, 31, 32, 48); what they can redeem (Le 25:26); when (Le 25:26, 51, 52); and for how much (Le 25:26, 51, 52). Redemption was a means by which property remained in families or clans. The best picture of this custom in the Bible is Ru 4:6, 7.

1481. גּוּר, **gûwr,** *goor*; a primitive root; properly to *turn* aside from the road (for a lodging or any other purpose), i.e. *sojourn* (as a guest); also to *shrink, fear* (as in a *strange* place); also to *gather* for hostility (as *afraid*):—abide, assemble, be afraid, dwell, fear, gather (together), inhabitant, remain, sojourn, stand in awe, (be) stranger, × surely.

A verb meaning to sojourn, to dwell as a foreigner; in the reflexive sense, to seek hospitality with. The term is commonly used of the patriarchs who sojourned in Canaan (Ge 26:3; 35:27); places outside Canaan (Ge 12:10; 20:1; 21:23; 32:4[5]; 47:4); Naomi and her family in Moab (Ru 1:1); the exiles in Babylonia (Jer 42:15). Metaphorically, the term is used of one who worships in God's temple (Ps 15:1; 61:4[5]). It is used reflexively with the meaning to seek hospitality with in 1Ki 17:20.

1540. גָּלָה, **gâlâh,** *gaw-law´*; a primitive root; to *denude* (especially in a disgraceful sense); (by implication) to *exile* (captives being usually *stripped*); (figurative) to *reveal*:— + advertise, appear, bewray, bring, (carry, lead, go) captive (into captivity), depart, disclose, discover, exile, be gone, open, × plainly, publish, remove, reveal, × shamelessly, shew, × surely, tell, uncover.

A verb meaning to reveal, to be revealed, to uncover, to remove, to go into exile, to reveal oneself, to expose, to disclose. It is used with the words ear (1Sa 9:15; 20:2, 12, 13) and eyes (Nu 24:4), meaning to reveal. On occasion, it is used in the expression to uncover the nakedness of, which often implies sexual relations (Le 18:6)

ד (Daleth)
OT Numbers 1668–1886

1698. דֶּבֶר, **deber,** *deh´-ber*; from 1696 (in the sense of *destroying*); a *pestilence*:— murrain, pestilence, plague.

A noun meaning plague or pestilence. This plague is a dreaded disease similar to the bubonic plague in the Middle Ages. It was likely carried by rat fleas and produced tumors on the infected person. First Samuel 5—6 describes the plague on the Philistines as a punishment from God. The word is also used as the most dreaded threat of the Lord against His people (Le 26:25; Nu 14:12). The prophets use this word frequently to predict coming judgment and destruction as in the common phrase, sword, famine, and plague (Jer 21:9; 38:2; Eze 6:11, NIV).

ה (He)
OT Numbers 1887–2050

1949. הוּם, **hûwm,** *hoom*; a primitive root [compare 2000]; to *make an uproar*, or *agitate* greatly:—destroy, move, make a noise, put, ring again.

A verb meaning to rouse, to roar, to confuse. This verb describes a stirring or rousing, such as occurred in Bethlehem when Ruth and Naomi returned from Moab (Ru 1:19), or would occur in the nations when God would confuse them before their destruction (Dt 7:23). On several occasions, the audible effects of the rousing was emphasized, such as when Solomon was anointed king, the roar of the city could be heard (1Ki 1:45; cf. 1Sa 4:5; Mic 2:12). In the only other occurrence of this verb, David described himself as restless and roused (Ps 55:2[3]).

ז (Zayin)
OT Numbers 2061–2242

2233. זֶרַע, **zera',** *zeh'-rah*; from 2232; *seed*; (figurative) *fruit, plant, sowing-time, posterity*:— × carnally, child, fruitful, seed (-time), sowing-time.

A masculine noun meaning sowing, seed, descendants, offspring, children, and posterity. The literal use of the word indicates seed of the field (i.e. seed planted in the field). When Israel entered Egypt, Joseph instructed the Israelites to keep four-fifths of the crop as seed to plant in their fields and to serve as food for them (Ge 47:24); the season for planting seed was guaranteed by God to continue without fail (Ge 8:22); and successful, abundant harvests were promised right up until the sowing season if Israel followed the Lord's laws and commands (Le 26:5). God had created the seed of the field by decreeing that plants and trees would be self-perpetuating, producing their own seed (Ge 1:11) and that the seed-producing plants would be edible (Ge 1:29). Manna, the heavenly food, resembled coriander seed (Ex 16:31). Any seed could be rendered unclean and not usable if a dead body fell on it after the seed had been moistened (Le 11:38).

The noun is used to describe the seed (i.e. the offspring) of both people and animals. The seed of Judah and Israel would be united and planted peacefully in the land together with animals in a pleasant setting (Jer 31:27). Seed can be translated as son (i.e. seed as when God gives Hannah a promise of a son [1Sa 1:11]). The seed of a woman mentioned in Ge 3:15 is her offspring.

The offspring of humans is described many times by this word. Hannah was given additional children to replace Samuel, whom she gave to the Lord's service (1Sa 2:20). The most important seed that the author of Genesis describes is the seed of Abraham, the promised seed, referring to Isaac, Jacob, and his twelve sons (Ge 12:7; 15:3). The author of Genesis uses the word twenty-one times in this setting (Ex 32:13; Dt 1:8). The seed of the royal line of David was crucial to Israel's existence, and the term is used nine times to refer to David's offspring or descendants (2Sa 7:12). In a figurative sense, seed refers to King Zedekiah and perhaps to Israelites of royal lineage, whom Nebuchadnezzar established in Jerusalem (Eze 17:5). Royal lines or seed were found outside Israel, such as in Edom, where Hadad belonged to the royal line (1Ki 11:14), and in Judah, where the wicked Athaliah attempted to destroy the royal seed (2Ki 11:1; 25:25; Jer 41:1).

The seed or offspring of a particular nation can be characterized in moral and religious terms as well. Three verses stand out: The seed of Israel was called a holy seed (Ezr 9:2; Isa 6:13); and, in the case of Ezr 9:2, the seed corrupted itself by mixing with the peoples around them. The seed of Israel is a seed of God or a divine seed (Mal 2:15) through its union with God (cf. 2Pe 1:4). An offspring could be described as deceitful and wicked (Ps 37:28; Isa 57:4). It was important in Israel to prove that one's origin or seed stemmed from an Israelite ancestor, for some Israelites and Israelite priests who returned from exile could not show their origin (Ezr 2:59). The word also refers to the seed or posterity of the Messiah (Isa 53:10).

ח (Heth)
OT Numbers 2243–2867

2416. חַי, **chay,** *khah′ee*; from 2421; *alive*; hence *raw* (flesh); *fresh* (plant, water, year), *strong*; also (as noun, especially in the feminine singular and masculine plural) *life* (or living thing), whether literal or figurative:— + age, alive, appetite, (wild) beast, company, congregation, life (-time), live (-ly), living (creature, thing), maintenance, + merry, multitude, + (be) old, quick, raw, running, springing, troop.

A feminine noun meaning a living thing, an animal, a beast, a living thing. The basic meaning is living things, but its most common translation is animals or beasts. The word refers to all kinds of animals and beasts of the field or earth (Ge 1:24, 25; 1Sa 17:46) and sometimes stands in parallel with birds of the air (Eze 29:5). The nations, such as Egypt, were referred to metaphorically as beasts (Ps 68:30[31]). Beasts were categorized in various ways: beasts of burden (Isa 46:1); land animals (Ge 1:28; 8:19); cattle (Nu 35:3); sea creatures (Ps 104:25); clean, edible creatures (Le 11:47; 14:4); unclean, nonedible creatures (Le 5:2); large and small creatures (Ps 104:25).

Two further categories of animals are noted: wild animals or animals of prey and animal or beastlike beings. God made the wild animals of the field. Sometimes the Lord used wild beasts as instruments of His judgments (Eze 14:15; 33:27), but on other occasions He protected His people from ravenous beasts (Ge 37:20; Le 26:6). At any rate, vicious beasts will not inhabit the land of the Lord's restored people (Isa 35:9). The bizarre living beings mentioned in Eze 1:5, 13, 22; 3:13 were like birds and animals but were composite beings. They could not be described adequately by human language, for they also had the forms of humans, each with faces of a man, lion, ox, and eagle. However, they did not resemble flesh and blood in their appearance (Eze 1:13) and were tied to the movement of the Spirit (Eze 1:20).

2428. חַיִל, **chayil,** *khah′-yil*; from 2342; probably a *force*, whether of men, means or other resources; an *army, wealth, virtue, valor, strength*:—able, activity, (+) army, band of men (soldiers), company, (great) forces, goods, host, might, power, riches, strength, strong, substance, train, (+) valiant (-ly), valour, virtuous (-ly), war, worthy (-ily).

A masculine noun meaning strength, wealth, army. This word has the basic idea of strength and influence. It can be used to speak of the strength of people (1Sa 2:4; 9:1; 2Sa 22:40); of horses (Ps 33:17); or of nations (Est 1:3). God is often seen as the supplier of this strength (2Sa 22:33; Hab 3:19). When describing men, it can speak of those who are strong for war (Dt 3:18; 2Ki 24:16; Jer 48:14); able to judge (Ex 18:21, 25); or are righteous in behavior (1Ki 1:52). When describing women, it speaks of virtuous character (Ru 3:11; Pr 12:4; 31:10). This idea of strength often is used to imply a financial influence (i.e. wealth) (Job 31:25; Ps 49:6[7]; Zec 14:14); a military influence (i.e. an army) (Ex 14:9; 2Ch 14:8[7], 9[8]; Isa 43:17); or a numerical influence (i.e. a great company) (1Ki 10:2; 2Ch 9:1).

2617. חֶסֶד, **chêsêd**, *kheh'-sed*; from 2616; *kindness*; by implication (toward God) *piety*; rarely (by opposition) *reproof*, or (subjective) *beauty*:—favour, good deed (-liness, -ness), kindly, (loving-) kindness, merciful (kindness), mercy, pity, reproach, wicked thing.

A masculine noun indicating kindness, lovingkindness, mercy, goodness, faithfulness, love, acts of kindness. This aspect of God is one of several important features of His character: truth; faithfulness; mercy; steadfastness; justice; righteousness; goodness. The classic text for understanding the significance of this word is Ps 136 where it is used twenty-six times to proclaim that God's kindness and love are eternal. The psalmist made it clear that God's kindness and faithfulness serves as the foundation for His actions and His character: it underlies His goodness (Ps 136:1); it supports His unchallenged position as God and Lord (Ps 136:2, 3); it is the basis for His great and wondrous acts in creation (Ps 136:4–9) and delivering and redeeming His people from Pharaoh and the Red Sea (Ps 136:10–15); the reason for His guidance in the desert (Ps 136:16); His gift of the land to Israel and defeat of their enemies (Ps 136:17–22); His ancient as well as His continuing deliverance of His people (Ps 136:23–25); His rulership in heaven (Ps 136:26). The entire span of creation to God's redemption, preservation, and permanent establishment is touched upon in this psalm. It all happened, is happening, and will continue to happen because of the Lord's covenant faithfulness and kindness.

The other more specific uses of the term develop the ideas contained in Ps 136 in greater detail. Because of His kindness, He meets the needs of His creation by delivering them from enemies and despair (Ge 19:19; Ex 15:13; Ps 109:26; Jer 31:3); He preserves their lives and redeems them from sin (Ps 51:1[3]; 86:13). As Ps 136 demonstrates, God's kindness is abundant, exceedingly great, without end, and good (Ex 34:6; Nu 14:19; Ps 103:8; 109:21; Jer 33:11). The plural of the noun indicates the many acts of God on behalf of His people (Ge 32:10[11]; Isa 63:7). He is the covenant-keeping God who maintains kindness and mercy (Dt 7:9) to those who love Him.

People are to imitate God. They are to display kindness and faithfulness toward each other (1Sa 20:15; Ps 141:5; Pr 19:22), especially toward the poor, weak, and needy (Job 6:14; Pr 20:28). Israel was to show kindness and faithfulness toward the Lord but often failed. In its youth, Israel showed faithfulness to God, but its devotion lagged later (Jer 2:2). It was not constant (Hos 6:4), appearing and leaving as the morning mist even though God desired this from His people more than sacrifices (Hos 6:6; cf. 1Sa 15:22). He looked for pious people (Isa 57:1) who would perform deeds of piety, faithfulness, and kindness (2Ch 32:32; 35:26; Ne 13:14); the Lord desired people who would maintain covenant loyalty and responsibility so that He could build His righteous community.

2620. חָסָה, **châsâh,** *khaw-saw´*; a primitive root; to *flee* for protection [compare 982]; (figurative) to *confide* in:—have hope, make refuge, (put) trust.

A verb meaning to seek, to take refuge. The word is used literally in reference to seeking a tree's shade (Jgs 9:15) and taking refuge in Zion (Isa 14:32). It is commonly used figuratively in relation to deities (Dt 32:37), particularly of Yahweh. He is a shield providing refuge (2Sa 22:31). Refuge is sought under His wings (Ru 2:12; Ps 36:7[8]; 57:1[2]; 61:4[5]; 91:4) and at the time of death (Pr 14:32).

2729. חָרַד, **chârad,** *khaw-rad´*; a primitive root; to *shudder* with terror; hence to *fear*; also to *hasten* (with anxiety):—be (make) afraid, be careful, discomfit, fray (away), quake, tremble.

A verb meaning to tremble, to quake, to be terrified. The term is used in reference to mountains (Ex 19:18); islands (Isa 41:5); birds and beasts (Jer 7:33); and people (Eze 32:10). It can mark a disturbance, such as being startled from sleep (Ru 3:8); or terror brought on by a trumpet's sound (Am 3:6); or an act of God (1Sa 14:15). It is often connected with terrifying an enemy in battle. It is also used in the causative, meaning to terrify (Jgs 8:12; 2Sa 17:2; Zec 1:21[2:4]). See the word *chărâdâh* (2731).

ט (Teth)
OT Numbers 2868–2967

2896. טוֹב, **ṭôwb,** *tobe*; from 2895; *good* (as an adjective) in the widest sense; used likewise as a noun, both in the masculine and the feminine, the singular and the plural (*good, a good* or *good* thing, a *good* man or woman; the *good, goods* or *good* things, *good* men or women), also as an adverb (*well*):—beautiful, best, better, bountiful, cheerful, at ease, × fair (word), (be in) favour, fine, glad, good (deed, -lier, -liest, -ly, -ness, -s), graciously, joyful, kindly, kindness, liketh (best), loving, merry, × most, pleasant, + pleaseth, pleasure, precious, prosperity, ready, sweet, wealth, welfare, (be) well ([-favoured]).

An adjective meaning good, well-pleasing, fruitful, morally correct, proper, convenient. This word is frequently encountered in the OT and is roughly equivalent to the English word *good* in terms of its function and scope of meaning. It describes that which is appealing and pleasant to the senses (Nu 14:7; Est 1:11; Ps 52:9[11]); is useful and profitable (Ge 2:18; Zec 11:12); is abundant and plentiful (Ge 41:22; Jgs 8:32); is kind and benevolent (1Sa 24:18[19]; 2Ch 5:13; Na 1:7); is good in a moral sense as opposed to evil (Ge 2:17; Le 27:14; Ps 37:27); is proper and becoming (Dt 1:14; 1Sa 1:23; Ps 92:1[2]); bears a general state of well-being or happiness (Dt 6:24; Ecc 2:24); is the better of two alternatives (Ge 29:19; Ex 14:12; Jnh 4:3). The creation narrative of Ge 1 best embodies all these various elements of meaning when the Lord declares each aspect of His handiwork to be "good."

י (Yodh)
OT Numbers 2968–3509

3045. יָדַע, **yâda',** *yaw-dah'*; a primitive root; to *know* (properly to ascertain by *seeing*); used in a great variety of senses, figurative, literal, euphemism and inference (including *observation, care, recognition*; and causative *instruction, designation, punishment*, etc.) [as follow]:—acknowledge, acquaintance (-ted with), advise, answer, appoint, assuredly, be aware, [un-] awares, can [-not], certainly, for a certainty, comprehend, consider, × could they, cunning, declare, be diligent, (can, cause to) discern, discover, endued with, familiar friend, famous, feel, can have, be [ig-] norant, instruct, kinsfolk, kinsman, (cause to, let, make) know, (come to give, have, take) knowledge, have [knowledge], (be, make, make to be, make self) known, + be learned, + lie by man, mark, perceive, privy to, × prognosticator, regard, have respect, skilful, shew, can (man of) skill, be sure, of a surety, teach, (can) tell, understand, have [understanding], × will be, wist, wit, wot.

A verb meaning to know, to learn, to perceive, to discern, to experience, to confess, to consider, to know people relationally, to know how, to be skillful, to be made known, to make oneself known, to make to know.

The simple meaning, to know, is its most common translation out of the eight hundred or more uses. One of the primary uses means to know relationally and experientially: it refers to knowing or not knowing persons (Ge 29:5; Ex 1:8) personally or by reputation (Job 19:13). The word also refers to knowing a person sexually (Ge 4:1; 19:5; 1Ki 1:4). It may even describe knowing or not knowing God or foreign gods (Ex 5:2; Dt 11:28; Hos 2:20[22]; 8:2), but it especially signifies knowing what to do or think in general, especially with respect to God (Isa 1:3; 56:10). One of its most important uses is depicting God's knowledge of people: The Lord knows their hearts entirely (Ex 33:12; 2Sa 7:20; Ps 139:4; Jer 17:9; Hos 5:3); God knows the suffering of His people (Ex 2:25), and He cares.

The word also describes knowing various other things: when Adam and Eve sinned, knowing good and evil (Ge 3:22); knowing nothing (1Sa 20:39); and knowing the way of wisdom (Job 28:23). One could know by observation (1Sa 23:22, 23), as when Israel and Pharaoh came to know God through the plagues He brought on Egypt (Ex 10:2). People knew by experience (Jos 23:14) that God kept His promises; this kind of experience could lead to knowing by confession (Jer 3:13; 14:20). Persons could be charged to know what they were about to do (Jgs 18:14) or what the situation implied (1Ki 20:7) so they would be able to discriminate between right and wrong, good and bad, what was not proper or advantageous (Dt 1:39; 2Sa 19:35[36]).

The word describes different aspects of knowing in its other forms. In the passive forms, it describes making something or someone known. The most famous illustration is Ex 6:3 when God asserted to Moses that He did not make himself known to the fathers as Yahweh.

‏כ‎ (Kaph)
OT Numbers 3510–3807

3772. ‏כָּרַת‎, kârath, *kaw-rath´*; a primitive root; to *cut* (off, down or asunder); (by implication) to *destroy* or *consume*; specifically to *covenant* (i.e. make an alliance or bargain, originally by cutting flesh and passing between the pieces):—be chewed, be con- [feder-] ate, covenant, cut (down, off), destroy, fail, feller, be freed, hew (down), make a league ([covenant]), × lose, perish, × utterly, × want.

A verb meaning to cut off, to cut down, to make a covenant. This word can mean literally to cut something down or off, as grapes (Nu 13:23, 24); or branches (Jgs 9:48, 49). It can also be used figuratively, as with people (Jer 11:19; 50:16). Another important use of this word is to make a covenant (lit., to cut a covenant), perhaps deriving from the practice of cutting an animal in two in the covenant ceremony. God made a covenant with Abraham (Ge 15:18); Abraham made one with Abimelech (Ge 21:27). Finally, this word can also mean to destroy, as in Micah's prophecy (Mic 5:10).

ל (Lamedh)
OT Numbers 3808–3963

3820. לֵב, **lêb,** *labe;* a form of 3824; the *heart;* also used (figurative) very widely for the feelings, the will and even the intellect; likewise for the *centre* of anything:— + care for, comfortably, consent, × considered, courag [-eous], friend [-ly], ([broken-], [hard-], [merry-], [stiff-], [stout-], double) heart ([-ed]), × heed, × I, kindly, midst, mind (-ed), × regard ([-ed]), × themselves, × unawares, understanding, × well, willingly, wisdom.

A masculine noun usually rendered as heart but whose range of meaning is extensive. It can denote the heart as a human physical organ (Ex 28:29; 1Sa 25:37; 2Ki 9:24); or an animal (Job 41:24[16]). However, it usually refers to some aspect of the immaterial inner self or being since the heart is considered to be the seat of one's inner nature as well as one of its components. It can be used in a general sense (1Ki 8:23; Ps 84:2[3]; Jer 3:10); or it can be used of a specific aspect of personality: the mind (Ge 6:5; Dt 29:4[3]; Ne 6:8); the will (Ex 35:5; 2Ch 12:14; Job 11:13); the emotions (Ge 6:6[Note that God is the subject]; 1Sa 24:5[6]; 25:31). In addition, the word can also allude to the inside or middle (Ex 15:8; Dt 4:11).

מ (Mem)
OT Numbers 3964–4993

4751. מַר, **mar,** *mar;* or (feminine) מָרָה, **mârâh,** *maw-raw´;* from 4843; *bitter* (literal or figurative); also (as noun) *bitterness,* or (adverb) *bitterly:*— + angry, bitter (-ly, -ness), chafed, discontented, × great, heavy.

A masculine adjective meaning bitter. The feminine form is *mârâh*. As is common with Hebrew adjectives, it can modify another noun (Ex 15:23), or it can be a substantive, functioning alone as the noun bitterness (Isa 38:15, 17). This word can also operate as an adverb, meaning bitterly (Isa 33:7; Eze 27:30). Used literally, it may modify water (Ex 15:23) and food (Pr 27:7). The Hebrew word can also be used to describe the results of continued fighting (2Sa 2:26). It can be used metaphorically to modify a cry or mourning (Ge 27:34; Est 4:1; Eze 27:30); to represent a characteristic of death (1Sa 15:32); or to describe a person as hot-tempered (Jgs 18:25); discontented (1Sa 22:2); provoked (2Sa 17:8); anguished (Eze 27:31); or ruthless (Hab 1:6). One instance of this word that deserves special attention is the "bitter water," that determined the legal status of a woman accused of infidelity (Nu 5:18, 19, 23, 24, 27). This was holy water that was combined with dust from the tabernacle floor and ink (see Nu 5:17, 23) and then was ingested by the accused. This water was literally "bitter" and would produce "bitterness" or punishment if the woman were guilty.

4755. מָרָא, **Mârâ'**, *maw-raw'*; for 4751 feminine; *bitter; Mara*, a symbolical name of Naomi:—Mara.

נ (Nun)
OT Numbers 4994–5428

5237. נָכְרִי, **nokrîy**, *nok-ree'*; from 5235 (second form); *strange*, in a variety of degrees and applications (*foreign, non-relative, adulterous, different, wonderful*):—alien, foreigner, outlandish, strange (-r, woman).

An adjective meaning strange, foreign, stranger, foreigner. It refers to someone who was not part of the family (Ge 31:15; cf. Ge 31:14; Ps 69:8[9]), especially the extended family of Israel (Dt 17:15). Under the Law, strangers were not allowed to rule in Israel (Dt 17:15); they were not released from their debts every seven years as Hebrews were (Dt 15:3); and could be sold certain ceremonially unclean food (Dt 14:21). Strangers were regarded as unholy (Dt 14:21); and were often looked down on (Ru 2:10; Job 19:15). Some hope for the conversion of foreigners was offered (Ru 2:10; 1Ki 8:41, 43); but with this word, more emphasis was placed on avoiding the defilement of foreign women (1Ki 11:1; Ezr 10:2, 10, 11, 14, 17, 18, 44; Pr 6:24); and foreign ways (Isa 2:6; Jer 2:21; Zep 1:8). The word *gêr* (1616), meaning sojourner, focuses more sympathetically on foreigners in Israel.

ע (Ayin)
OT Numbers 5645–6283

6172. עֶרְוָה, *'ervâh, er-vaw'*; from 6168; *nudity*, literal (especially the *pudenda*) or figurative (*disgrace, blemish*):—nakedness, shame, unclean(-ness).

A feminine noun expressing nakedness. This word can pertain to physical nakedness for either a man or a woman (Ge 9:22, 23; Ex 20:26); however, it is more often used in a figurative sense. When used with the verbs *gâlâh* (1540), meaning to uncover or remove, and *râ'âh* (7200), meaning to see, one finds a common euphemism for sexual relations—to uncover one's nakedness (Le 18:6; 20:17). On the other hand, when combined with the verb *kâsâh* (3680), meaning to cover, one finds a common idiom for entering into a marriage contract (Eze 16:8). Nakedness is also a symbol of the shame and disgrace of Egypt (Isa 20:4); Babylonia (Isa 47:3); and Jerusalem (Eze 16:37). Furthermore, when in construct with *dâbâr* (1697), meaning a word, matter, or thing, this term forms an idiom for indecent or improper behaviour (Dt 23:14[15]; 24:1). When in construct with the word *'erets* (776), it can refer to exposed or undefended areas (Ge 42:9, 12).

6213. עָשָׂה, *'âśâh, aw-saw'*; a primitive root; to *do* or *make*, in the broadest sense and widest application (as follows):—accomplish, advance, appoint, apt, be at, become, bear, bestow, bring forth, bruise, be busy, × certainly, have the charge of, commit, deal (with), deck, + displease, do, (ready) dress (-ed), (put in) execute (-ion), exercise, fashion, + feast, [fight-] ing man, + finish, fit, fly, follow, fulfil, furnish, gather, get, go about, govern, grant, great, + hinder, hold ([a feast]), × indeed, + be industrious, + journey, keep, labour, maintain, make, be meet, observe, be occupied, offer, + officer, pare, bring (come) to pass, perform, practise, prepare, procure, provide, put, requite, × sacrifice, serve, set, shew, × sin, spend, × surely, take, × throughly, trim, × very, + vex, be [warr-] ior, work (-man), yield, use.

A verb meaning to do, to make, to accomplish, to complete. This frequently used Hebrew verb conveys the central notion of performing an activity with a distinct purpose, a moral obligation, or a goal in view (cf. Ge 11:6). Particularly, it was used in conjunction with God's commands (Dt 16:12). It described the process of construction (Ge 13:4; Job 9:9; Pr 8:26); engaging in warfare (Jos 11:18); the yielding of grain (Hos 8:7); observing a religious ceremony (Ex 31:16; Nu 9:4); and the completion of something (Ezr 10:3; Isa 46:10). Provocatively, the word appears twice in Ezekiel to imply the intimate action of caressing or fondling the female breast (Eze 23:3, 8).

פ (Pe)
OT Numbers 6284–6626

6341. פַּח, **pach,** *pakh*; from 6351; a (metallic) *sheet* (as *pounded* thin); also a spring *net* (as spread out like a *lamina*):—gin, (thin) plate, snare.

A masculine singular noun translated bird trap. It is used in its literal sense in Am 3:5, Pr 7:23, and Ecc 9:12. But more often it is used figuratively for a human ensnarement. Jeremiah prophesied that a snare awaited Moab (Jer 48:43); while Proverbs said that snares were set for the wicked (Pr 22:5). Eliphaz told Job that snares surrounded him (Job 22:10). The psalmist's path was filled with the snares of his enemies (Ps 140:5[6]; 142:3[4]). But retribution was envisioned as the enemies' tables turned into a snare (Ps 69:22[23]).

צ (Tsadhe)
OT Numbers 6627–6891

6680. צָוָה, **tsâvâh,** *tsaw-vaw´*; a primitive root; (intensive) to *constitute, enjoin:*—appoint, (for-) bid, (give a) charge, (give a, give in, send with) command (-er, -ment), send a messenger, put, (set) in order.

A verb meaning to order, to direct, to appoint, to command, to charge, to be ordered, to be commanded. The word means to give an order or to command, to direct someone; it indicates commands given to people in various situations. The Lord commanded Adam and Eve to eat from certain trees but to refrain from eating from the tree of the knowledge of good and evil (Ge 2:16; 3:17). He ordered Moses hundreds of times to do or say certain things as He established Israel's worship, feasts, festivals, and rituals (Ex 7:2; 16:34; Nu 15:23). Israel was to keep all the directives the Lord gave them (Dt 4:2; 1Ki 11:10). The Lord commanded His prophets to speak (Am 6:11; Na 1:14; Zec 1:6). People gave orders to others as well, as when Pharaoh ordered that all newborn Hebrew males should be drowned in the Nile River (Ex 1:22). Deborah ordered Barak to defeat Sisera (Jgs 4:6). Abraham ordered his family to follow the ways of the Lord (Ge 18:19). Kings commanded their people (1Ki 5:17[31]; Jer 36:26). Priests in Israel gave directives to the people about what to do under certain circumstances (Le 9:6; cf. Le 13:58). A person who was chosen for a task or position was commanded concerning his responsibilities by the priestly authorities (Nu 27:19, 23). The word may mean to give directives or to set in order as when the Lord told Hezekiah to order—that is, to set things in order, in his household, for he was about to die (2Ki 20:1).

God commands not only people but creation: He created all things by His command (Ps 33:9; 148:5); He commanded the clouds not to send their rain on a disobedient vineyard (i.e. Israel [Ps 78:23; Isa 5:6]); He commands the entire heavenly realms (Isa 45:12). God commands historical processes; He will ultimately set up David, His ruler, as the one who commands (Isa 55:4).

ר (Resh)
OT Numbers 7200–7578

7200. רָאָה, **râ'âh**, *raw-aw'*; a primitive root; to *see*, literal or figurative (in numerous applications, direct and implied, transitive, intransitive and causative):—advise self, appear, approve, behold, × certainly, consider, discern, (make to) enjoy, have experience, gaze, take heed, × indeed, × joyfully, lo, look (on, one another, one on another, one upon another, out, up, upon), mark, meet, × be near, perceive, present, provide, regard, (have) respect, (fore-, cause to, let) see (-r, -m, one another), shew (self), × sight of others, (e-) spy, stare, × surely, × think, view, visions.

A verb meaning to see. Its basic denotation is to see with the eyes (Ge 27:1). It can also have the following derived meanings, all of which require the individual to see physically outside of himself or herself: to see so that one can learn to know, whether it be another person (Dt 33:9) or God (Dt 1:31; 11:2); to experience (Jer 5:12; 14:13; 20:18; 42:14); to perceive (Ge 1:4, 10, 12, 18, 21, 25, 31; Ex 3:4); to see by volition (Ge 9:22, 23; 42:9, 12); to look after or to visit (Ge 37:14; 1Sa 20:29); to watch (1Sa 6:9); to find (1Sa 16:17); to select (2Ki 10:3); to be concerned with (Ge 39:23). It is also possible for this verb to require the individual to make a mental observation. As an imperative, it can function as an exclamation similar to *hinnêh* (2009), which means to behold (Ge 27:27; 31:50). Further, it can denote to give attention to (Jer 2:31); to look into or inquire (1Sa 24:15[16]); to take heed (Ex 10:10); to discern (Ecc 1:16; 3:13); to distinguish (Mal 3:18); to consider or reflect on (Ecc 7:14). It can also connote a spiritual observation and comprehension by means of seeing visions (Ge 41:22; Isa 30:10).

7210. רֳאִי, **ro'îy**, *ro-ee'*; from 7200; *sight*, whether abstract (*vision*) or concrete (a *spectacle*):—gazing-stock, look to, (that) see (-th).

A masculine noun meaning sight, an appearance, a spectacle. The basic force of this word is that of a visible appearance. It is used in reference to God's ability to see (Ge 16:13); the outward look of an individual (1Sa 16:12); and a visual spectacle that drew attention to itself (Na 3:6).

שׂ (Sin/Shin)
OT Numbers 7579–8371

7673. שָׁבַת, **shâbath,** *shaw-bath´*; a primitive root; to *repose,* i.e. *desist* from exertion; used in many implication relations (causative, figurative or specific):—(cause to, let, make to) cease, celebrate, cause (make) to fail, keep (sabbath), suffer to be lacking, leave, put away (down), (make to) rest, rid, still, take away.

A verb meaning to repose, to rest, to rid of, to still, to put away, to leave. Most often, the word expresses the idea of resting (i.e. abstaining from labour), especially on the seventh day (see Ex 20:8–11). It is from this root that the noun for *Sabbath* originates, a word designating the time to be set aside for rest. The verb is used of God to describe His resting after the completion of creation (Ge 2:2). This example of rest by God at creation set the requirement of rest that He desires for His people in order that they may live lives pleasing to Him, full of worship and adoration (Ex 31:17). In Joshua, the verb expresses a cessation of the provision of manna by God to the Israelites (Jos 5:12). The land was also depicted as enjoying a rest from the Israelite farmers while they were in exile (Le 26:34, 35).

Daniel uses this verb to indicate a ceasing of ritual sacrifice and offerings (Da 9:27). In that passage, Daniel was speaking of the Messiah's coming and the establishment of the New Covenant, when there would be no more need for ritual sacrifices. In another context, the verb can mean to exterminate or destroy a certain object, such as in Am 8:4 in which Amos addresses those who trampled the needy and did away with the poor. The verb means to cause, to desist from, as in God's declaration of action against the shepherds (Eze 34:10). The word suggests a removing of people or other objects (Ex 12:15; Eze 23:27, 48; Isa 30:11). In still other contexts, the causative stem means to fail or to leave lacking. In Ru 4:14, God was praised because He did not leave Naomi without a kinsman-redeemer.

7706. שַׁדַּי, **Shadday,** *shad-dah´ee*; from 7703; the *Almighty:*—Almighty.

A masculine noun and name for God meaning Shaddai, Almighty. The word occurs only forty-eight times in the Hebrew Bible, thirty-one times in the book of Job. This is a name for the Lord—the OT people of faith referring to Him as El Shaddai, God Almighty. The term is found in the passages that report God's promises of fertility, land, and abundance to them, indicating that He, the Almighty, could fulfill His promises (Ge 17:1; 28:3; 35:11). The Lord appeared to Abraham when he was ninety-nine years old and identified himself as El Shaddai, God Almighty (Ge 17:1). All three patriarchs knew

Him by this name (Ge 28:1–3; 35:11); as did Joseph (Ge 48:3; cf. Ex 6:3); Ezekiel the prophet knew the tradition of Shaddai as well (Eze 10:5). Balaam, Naomi, the psalmist, Joel, and Isaiah employed the term Shaddai, Almighty (Nu 24:4; Ru 1:20; Ps 68:14[15]; Isa 13:6; Joel 1:15). But it is especially Job who uses the term appropriately as a non-Israelite (Job 5:17; 13:3; 24:1; 37:23), since it is a universal term for God. It is always found in poetic sections of material. The book of Job also uses the name the LORD, Yahweh, twenty-seven times, and it is found all but five times in the prose sections (Job 1—2; 42:7–17; see concordance for specific references).

7725. שׁוּב, **shûwb**, *shoob*; a primitive root; to *turn* back (hence, away) transitive or intransitive, literal or figurative (not necessarily with the idea of *return* to the starting point); (generally) to *retreat*; (often adverbial) *again*:— ([break, build, circumcise, dig, do anything, do evil, feed, lay down, lie down, lodge, make, rejoice, send, take, weep]) × again, (cause to) answer (+ again), × in any case (wise), × at all, averse, bring (again, back, home again), call [to mind], carry again (back), cease, × certainly, come again (back) × consider, + continually, convert, deliver (again), + deny, draw back, fetch home again, × fro, get [oneself] (back) again, × give (again), go again (back, home), [go] out, hinder, let, [see] more, × needs, be past, × pay, pervert, pull in again, put (again, up again), recall, recompense, recover, refresh, relieve, render (again), requite, rescue, restore, retrieve, (cause to, make to) return, reverse, reward, + say nay, send back, set again, slide back, still, × surely, take back (off), (cause to, make to) turn (again, self again, away, back, back again, backward, from, off), withdraw.

A verb meaning to turn, to return, to go back, to do again, to change, to withdraw, to bring back, to reestablish, to be returned, to bring back, to take, to restore, to recompense, to answer, to hinder. The verb is used over one thousand times and has various shades of meaning in its four stems. In the simple stem, it is used to describe divine and human reactions, attitudes, and feelings. The verb describes the possibility that Israel might change (turn) their minds and return to Egypt (Ex 13:17). Josiah the king turned back to the Lord with all his heart, soul, and strength (2Ki 23:25; Jer 34:15). Nevertheless, the Lord did not turn from the anger He held toward Judah (2Ki 23:26; Jer 4:28). Job pleaded with his miserable comforters to relent (i.e. turn away) from him (Job 6:29). God's people will return (repent) and seek Him in the last days (Dt 30:2; Isa 59:20; Hos 3:5) instead of turning away from Him as they are now; to return to Egypt (Isa 6:10; Hos 11:5). God's call was persistently for His people to return to Him (1Ki 8:33; Jer 4:1). Any nation can repent and turn to God for forgiveness (Jer 18:8).

The word is used metaphorically to describe things returning: God's Word will not be revoked (returned) once it has been uttered (Isa 45:23; 55:11); Jacob stayed with Laban until Esau's anger cooled off (turned back) (Ge 27:44, 45); blood guilt could return on one's own head (1Ki 2:33; Ps 7:16[17]). This word also describes the sword of Saul that did not return without success from the battlefield (2Sa 1:22).

The verb also indicates to returning to or to change into. For example, human beings return to the dust of the earth (Ge 3:19; Ecc 12:7); but a person cannot naturally return to life (2Sa 12:23); unless God's Spirit brings it about (1Ki 13:6). A land of great natural fertility can be reduced (turned into) to a farmer's cropland (Isa 29:17).*

In its simplest sense, the word means to return, to restore, to go back. Abraham's descendants in their fourth generation would return to Canaan (Ge 15:16); God returned to visit His people (Ge 8:9; 18:10). It is also used to describe turning chariots about when needed (1Ki 22:33; Mic 2:8).

This verb is used with other verbs of motion, all in their infinitive or participial forms, to describe a back and forth motion; the ravens Noah sent out went back and forth (Ge 8:7). Used with another verb in general, *shûb* is either not translated or means to do again whatever action is indicated by the other verb, such as when Isaac dug again the wells his father had previously dug (Ge 26:18). A similar meaning is to take back or recapture when this verb is used with the Hebrew verb *lâqach* (3947), meaning to take or to receive (2Ki 13:25; Mic 7:19). Finally, if this verb is used with a following infinitive of another verb, it means to do over and over or more and more; Israel angered the Lord more and more than they had already angered Him by performing pagan rituals (Eze 8:17).

NEW TESTAMENT DICTIONARY

**Taken from
AMG's Annotated
Strong's Greek Dictionary
Of the New Testament**

Additional materials in this dictionary were taken from
The Complete Word Study Dictionary: New Testament
compiled by Spiros Zodhiates.
©1992 by AMG Publishers. All Rights Reserved.

Transliteration of Greek Alphabet

Capital Letter	Lowercase Letter	Greek Name	Trans– literation	Phonetic Sound	Example
A	α	alpha	a	a	as in father
B	β	bēta	b	v	as in victory
Γ	γ	gamma	g	y	as in yell (soft gutteral)
Δ	δ	delta	d	th	as in there
E	ε	epsilon	e	e	as in met
Z	ζ	zēta	z	z	as in zebra
H	η	ēta	ē	ee	as in see
Θ	θ	thēta	th	th	as in thin
I	ι	iōta	i	i	as in machine
K	κ	kappa	k	k	as in kill (soft accent)
Λ	λ	lambda	l	l	as in land
M	μ	mē	m	m	as in mother
N	ν	nē	n	n	as in now
Ξ	ξ	xi	x	x	as in wax
O	ο	omicron	o	o	as in obey
Π	π	pi	p	p	as in pet (soft accent)
P	ρ	ro	r	r	as in courage
Σ	σ, ς*	sigma	s	s	as in sit
T	τ	tau	t	t	as in tell (soft accent)
Υ	υ	ēpsilon	u	ee	as in see
Φ	φ	phi	ph	ph	as in graphic
X	χ	chi	ch	h	as in heel
Ψ	ψ	psi	ps	ps	as in ships
Ω	ω	omega	ō	o	as in obey

*At the end of words

Combinations of Consonants

γγ	gamma + gamma	gg	g	as in go
γκ	gamma + kappa	gk	g	as in go
γχ	gamma + chi	gch	gh	as in ghost
μπ	mē + pi	mp	b	as in boy
ντ	nē + tau	nt	d	as in dog
τζ	tau + zēta	tz	g	as in gym

Transliteration of Greek Alphabet

Diphthongs (double vowels)

αι	alpha + iōta	ai	ai	as in hair
αυ	alpha + ēpsilon	au	af, av	as in waft or lava
ει	epsilon + iōta	ei	ee	as in see
ευ	epsilon + ēpsilon	eu	ef, ev	as in effort or every
ηυ	ēta + ēpsilon	ēu	eef, eev	as in reef or sleeve
οι	omicron + iōta	oi	ee	as in see
ου	omicron + epsilon	ou	ou	as in group
υι	epsilon + iōta	ui	ee	as in see

Breathing Marks

The smooth breathing mark (') is not transliterated or pronounced. When words begin with vowels, it may occur at the beginning of words with every vowel or double vowel (diphthong). ἔργον—*ergon*, work; εὐχή—*euchē*, vow.

The rough breathing mark (') is represented by an "h" in the transliteration. When words begin with vowels, it may occur at the beginning of words with every vowel or double vowel (diphthong). In modern Greek there is no distinction in pronunciation from the smooth breathing.

When rho or ēpsilon begin a word, they always have the rough breathing. There they are transliterated rh, hu, respectively. ῥέω—*rheō*, flow; ὑπομονή—*hupomonē*, patience.

Special Symbols

:— (colon and one-em dash) are used within each entry to mark the end of the discussion of syntax and meaning of the word under consideration, and to mark the beginning of the list of word(s) used to render it in translation.

() (parentheses) denote, in the translation renderings only, a word or syllable given in connection with the principal word it follows.

+ (addition symbol) denotes a rendering in translation of one or more Hebrew words in connection with the one under consideration.

× (multiplication symbol) denotes a rendering within translation that results from an idiom peculiar to the Greek.

A—Alpha
NT Numbers 1–895

553. ἀπεκδέχομαι, **apekdechomai,** *ap-ek-dekh´-om-ahee*; from 575 and 1551; to *expect fully*:—look (wait) for.

From *apó* (575), an intensive, and *ekdéchomai* (1551), to expect, look for. To wait out, i.e. to wait long for, to await ardently, to expect (Ro 8:19, 23, 25; 1Co 1:7; Gal 5:5; Php 3:20; Heb 9:28 [cf. 1Pe 3:20]).

Syn.: *prosdokáō* (4328), to await, expect; *prosdéchomai* (4327), to expect, look for; *anaménō* (362), to wait for with patience and confident expectancy; *periménō* (4037), to wait around for the fulfillment of an event; *proskarteréō* (4342), to wait around looking forward to the fulfillment of something one expects to take place; *elpízō* (1679), to hope; *prosménō* (4357), to tarry, wait with patience and steadfastness; *apoblépō* (578), to look away

728. ἀῤῥαβών, **arrhabōn,** *ar-hrab-ohn´*; of Hebrew origin [6162]; a *pledge*, i.e. part of the purchase money or property given in advance as *security* for the rest:—earnest.

Noun transliterated from the Hebrew *ʿarabōn* (6162, OT). Earnest money, a pledge given to ratify a contract (Sept.: Ge 38:17, 18, 20). In the NT, used metaphorically, spoken of the privileges of Christians in this life, especially the gift of the Holy Spirit, as being an earnest, a pledge of future bliss in the Messiah's kingdom (2Co 1:22; 5:5; Eph 1:14).

Syn.: *aparché* (536), translated "firstfruits"; *parakatathékē* (3872), a deposit.

Γ (Gamma)
NT Numbers 1042–1137

1131. γυμνός, **gumnos,** *goom-nos´*; of uncertain affinity; *nude* (absolute or relative, literal or figurative):—naked.

(I) In respect to the body: wholly nude, without any clothing (perhaps Mk 14:51, 52; figuratively, Rev 16:15; 17:16); also spoken of one who has no outer garment and is clad only in a tunic, which is fitted close to the body (Jn 21:7; Ac 19:16; probably Mk 14:51; Sept.: 1Sa 19:24; Isa 20:2). As in Eng., half-naked, i.e. poorly clad, destitute as to clothing, implying poverty and want (Mt 25:36, 38, 43, 44; Jas 2:15; Sept.: Job 31:19; 24:7; Isa 58:7). Figuratively: destitute of spiritual goods (Rev 3:17).

(II) Figuratively spoken of the soul as disencumbered of the body in which it had been clothed (2Co 5:3, cf. v. 4 and 15:51).

(III) Spoken of any thing as taken alone, abstractly, separate from everything else: naked, mere, bare (1Co 15:37).

(IV) Metaphorically: uncovered, open, manifest (Heb 4:13).

Deriv.: *gumnázō* (1128), to exercise; *gumnēteúō* (1130), to be naked or scantily clothed; *gumnótēs* (1132), nakedness, lack of sufficient clothing, metaphorically lack of spirituality

Ε (Epsilon)
NT Numbers 1436–2193

1656. ἔλεος, **eleos,** *el´-eh-os*; of uncertain affinity; *compassion* (human or divine, especially active):—(+ tender) mercy.

A noun meaning mercy, compassion:

(I) *Ho éleos*, gen. *éleou*, masc. noun:

(A) Mercy, compassion, active pity (Mt 23:23; Tit 3:5; Heb 4:16; Sept.: Isa 60:10).

(B) With the sense of goodness in general, especially piety (Mt 9:13; 12:7 quoted from Hos 6:6).

(II) *To éleos*, gen. *eléous*, neuter noun, found only in the Sept., the NT, and church writers in contrast to the noun in the masc. *ho éleos* which alone is used by Class. Gr. writers. Mercy, compassion, active pity:

(A) Generally (Lk 1:50, 78; Ro 9:23; 15:9; Eph 2:4; 1Pe 1:3; Jas 3:17; Sept.: Dt 13:17; Ne 13:22; Ps 51:1; Isa 63:7). With the verb *poiéō* (4160), to do mercy for someone, meaning to show mercy to, equivalent to the verb *eleéō* (1653), to have compassion on, show mercy (Lk 1:72; 10:37; Jas 2:13; Sept.: Ge 24:12; 1Sa 15:6). With the verb *megalúnō* (3170), to make great, magnify, show great mercy on someone (Lk 1:58). In the phrase, *mnēsthḗnai eléous*, lit. "to remember mercy" (from *mimnḗskō* [3403], to remember), meaning to give a new proof of mercy and favour to Israel, in reference to God's ancient mercies to that people (Lk 1:54 [cf. Ps 25:6; 89:28, 50; Sept.: 2Ch 6:42; Jer 2:2]). Spoken of mercy as a passing over of deserved punishment (Jas 2:13 [cf. Sept.: Nu 14:19]).

(B) Spoken of the mercy of God through Christ, i.e. salvation in the Christian sense from sin and misery (Jude 21, "the mercy of our Lord Jesus Christ" means salvation through Christ; see Ro 11:31). In benedictions, including the idea of mercies and blessings of every kind, e.g., "the Lord give mercy" (2Ti 1:16, 18). Also joined with *eirḗnē* (1515), peace (Gal 6:16; 1Ti 1:2; 2Ti 1:2; Tit 1:4; 2Jn 3; Jude 2).

Deriv.: *eleeinós* (1652), worthy of pity; *eleéō*

Λ (Lambda)
NT Numbers 2975–3091

3017. Λευΐ, **Leuï,** *lyoo-ee´*; of Hebrew origin [3878]; *Levi*, the name of three Israelites:— Levi. Compare 3018.

3056. λόγος, **logos,** *log´-os*; from 3004; something *said* (including the *thought*); (by implication) a *topic* (subject of discourse), also *reasoning* (the mental faculty or *motive*; by extension a *computation*; specially (with the art. in John) the Divine *Expression* (i.e. *Christ*):—account, cause, communication, × concerning, doctrine, fame, × have to do, intent, matter, mouth, preaching, question, reason, + reckon, remove, say (-ing), shew, × speaker, speech, talk, thing, + none of these things move me, tidings, treatise, utterance, word, work.

Noun from *légō* (3004), to speak intelligently. A word, as spoken; anything spoken; also reason as manifesting itself in the power of speech:

(**I**) A word, both the act of speaking and the thing spoken:

(**A**) A word, as uttered by the living voice, a speaking, speech, utterance (Mt 8:8; Lk 7:7; 23:9; 1Co 14:9; Heb 12:19); a saying, discourse, conversation (Mt 12:37; 15:12; 19:22; 22:15; 26:1; Ac 5:24). Metonymically, the power of speech, delivery, oratory, eloquence (1Co 12:8; 2Co 11:6; Eph 6:19). The Word of God, meaning His omnipotent voice, decree (2Pe 3:5, 7; Sept.: Ps 32:6 [cf. Ge 1:3; Ps 148:5]).

(**B**) A saying, declaration, sentiment uttered: (**1**) Generally (Mt 10:14; Lk 4:22; 20:20; Jn 6:60). In reference to words or declarations, e.g., which precede (Mt 7:24, 26; Mk 7:29; Jn 2:22; 6:60; 7:40; 10:19; 12:38; Ac 5:24; 20:35; Ro 9:9; 13:9; 1Co 15:54; 1Ti 3:1; Tit 3:8; Rev 19:9). The word, declaration of a prophet, meaning prediction, prophecy (Lk 3:4; Jn 12:38; Ac 15:15; 2Pe 1:19; Rev 1:3); a proverb, maxim (Jn 4:37). (**2**) In reference to religion, religious duties, i.e. doctrine, precept (Ac 15:24; 18:15; 1Ti 4:6; Tit 1:9; Heb 2:2); especially of God, the Word of God, meaning divine revelation and declaration, oracle (Mk 7:13; Lk 5:1; Jn 5:38; 10:35; 17:6; Ac 4:29; Ro 9:6, 28; 1Co 14:36; 2Co 4:2; Col 1:25; 1Th 2:13; Tit 1:3; Heb 4:2, 12; 13:7).

(**II**) Reason, the reasoning faculty as that power of the soul which is the basis of speech. In the NT:

(**A**) A reason, ground, cause (Mt 5:32; Ac 10:29; 18:14).

(**B**) Reason as demanded or assigned, i.e. a reckoning, an account (Mt 18:23; 25:19; Lk 16:2; Ac 19:40; 20:24; Heb 13:17; 1Pe 3:15; 4:5).

(III) The Word, the *Lógos* in the writings of John (Jn 1:1, 14; 1Jn 1:1; Rev 19:13); it here stands for the preexistent nature of Christ, i.e. that spiritual and divine nature spoken of in the Jewish writings before and about the time of Christ, under various names, e.g., Son of Man (Da 7:13); Word of Jehovah (used in the Aramaic Targums, the translations which were used in the Jewish synagogues along with the Hebrew Scriptures). On this divine word, the Jews of that age would appear to have had much subtle discussion; and therefore probably the apostle sets out with affirming, "In the beginning was the Word, and the Word was with God, and the Word was God" (Jn 1:1); and then also declares that this Word became flesh and was thus the Messiah (Jn 1:14).

Deriv.: *álogos* (249), irrational, without intelligence; *analogía* (356), analogy; *analogízomai* (357), to contemplate, consider; *apologéomai* (626), to answer back, defend oneself; *battologéō* (945), to use vain repetitions; *ellogéō* (1677), to account, reckon in; *eulogéō* (2127), to speak well of, bless; *logízomai* (3049), to reckon, impute; *logikós* (3050), reasonable; *lógios* (3052), fluent, orator, intelligent person; *polulogía* (4180), much speaking.

Syn.: *rhḗma* (4487), word, utterance. Also, *aggelía* (31), message, announcement; *eperṓtēma* (1906), an inquiry, answer; *laliá* (2981), speech; *homilía* (3657), homily, communication, speech; *propheteía* (4394), prophecy, something spoken ahead of its occurrence or spoken forth; *suzḗtēsis* (4803), mutual questioning; *phḗmē* (5345), fame, report, that which is being said about someone.

M (Mu)
NT Numbers 3092–3475

3144. μάρτυς, **martus**, *mar´-toos*; of uncertain affinity; a *witness* (literal [judicially] or figurative [genitive]); (by analogy) a "*martyr*":— martyr, record, witness.

(I) Particularly, in a judicial sense (Mt 18:16; 26:65; Mk 14:63; Ac 6:13; 7:58; 2Co 13:1; Heb 10:28).

(II) Generally, one who testifies or can testify to the truth of what he has seen, heard, knows (Ro 1:9; 2Co 1:23; Php 1:8; 1Th 2:10; 1Ti 6:12); so in allusion to those who witness a public game (Heb 12:1). Especially of those who witnessed the life, death, and resurrection of Jesus, who bear witness to the truth as it is in Jesus (Lk 24:48; Ac 1:8, 22; 2:32; 5:32; 26:16; 2Ti 2:2); so of one who bears witness for God, and testifies to the world what God reveals through him, i.e. a teacher, prophet (Rev 1:5; 3:14; 11:3).

(III) A martyr, one who by his death bears witness to the truth (Ac 22:20; Rev 2:13; 17:6).

Deriv.: *amárturos* (267), without a witness; *marturéō* (3140), to witness; *martúromai* (3143),

Π (Pi)
NT Numbers 3802–4459

4053. περισσός, **perissos,** *per-is-sos´*; from 4012 (in the sense of *beyond*); *superabundant* (in quantity) or *superior* (in quality); (by implication) *excessive*; adverb (with 1537) *violently*; neuter (as noun) *preeminence*:—exceeding abundantly above, more abundantly, advantage, exceedingly, very highly, beyond measure, more, superfluous, vehement [-ly].

Adjective from *perí* (4012), around, above. Over and above, more than enough.

(**I**) Particularly as exceeding a certain measure, more than (Mt 5:37, 47). In the sense of superfluous (2Co 9:1).

(**II**) Generally, superabundant, abundant, much, great.

(**A**) Positively, as an adverb, abundantly, in superabundance (Jn 10:10). With the prep. *ek* (1537), by means of, or expressing measure, beyond measure, exceedingly (Mk 6:51; 14:31; Eph 3:20; 1Th 3:10; 5:13).

(**B**) By implication, in a comparative sense, advantage (Ro 3:1).

Deriv.: *perisseía* (4050), a superfluity, an overflowing; *perisseúō* (4052), to abound, be exceeding.

X (Chi)
NT Numbers 5463–5566

5487. χαριτόω, **charitoō,** *khar-ee-to´-o*; from 5485; to *grace*, i.e. indue with special *honour*:—make accepted, be highly favoured.

From *cháris* (5485), grace. To bestow grace, highly honour or greatly favour. In the NT spoken only of the divine favour: to the virgin Mary (Lk 1:28); to all believers (Eph 1:6).

Ψ (Psi)
NT Numbers 5567–5597

5594. ψύχω, **psuchō,** *psoo´-kho*; a primary verb; to *breathe* (*voluntarily* but *gently*; thus differing on the one hand from 4154, which denotes properly a *forcible* respiration; and on the other from the base of 109, which refers properly to an inanimate *breeze*), i.e. (by implication of reduction of temperature by evaporation) to *chill* (figurative):—wax cold.

To breathe, blow, refresh with cool air, or breathe naturally. It is from this verb that *psuchḗ* (5590), soul, is derived. Hence *psuchḗ* is the breath of a living creature, animal life, and *psúchō* in the pass. *psúchomai*, means to be cool, to grow cool or cold in a spiritual sense, as in Christian love (Mt 24:12).

Deriv.: *anapsúchō* (404), to make cool, refresh; *apopsúchō* (674), to be faint of heart; *ekpsúchō* (1634), to expire, die; *katapsúchō* (2711), to cool off; *psuchḗ* (5590), soul; *psúchos*

HEBREW-GREEK KEY WORD® STUDY BIBLE

Editors: Dr. Spiros Zodhiates and Dr. Warren P. Baker

NEW KING JAMES VERSION
2648 pages • 7" x 9" • Carton Quantity: 8
Available in Hardcover Genuine Leather (Black & Burgundy)

ENGLISH STANDARD VERSION
2368 pages • 7" x 9" • Carton Quantity: 8
Available in Hardcover, Duraflex (Black) and Genuine Leather
(Black & Burgundy)

KING JAMES VERSION
2304 Pages • 7" x 9" • Carton Count: 8
Available in Hardcover, Bonded Leather Black & Burgundy) and
Genuine Leather (Black & Burgundy)

NEW AMERICAN STANDARD BIBLE (1977 EDITION)
2336 Pages • 7" x 9" • Carton Count: 8
Available in Hardcover, Bonded Leather Black & Burgundy) and
Genuine Leather (Black & Burgundy)

NEW INTERNATIONAL VERSION (1984 EDITION)
2108 Pages • 6.5" x 9" • Carton Count: 8
Available in Hardcover Bonded Leather (Black & Burgundy)

HEBREW-GREEK KEY WORD® STUDY BIBLE

Dr. Spiros Zodhiates' greatest contribution to Bible students everywhere is the *Hebrew-Greek Key Word® Study Bible*, which takes the reader to the source of the Hebrew and Greek words and Greek grammar. In addition, there are extensive exegetical footnotes explaining the most difficult passages of the Old and New Testaments.

FEATURES:
- New edition (**NKJV / KJV** Authorized Version / **NASB** 1977 ed. / **ESV** / **NIV** 1984 ed.)
- Wide **margins**
- **Introduction** to each book of the Bible
- Words of Christ in **RED**
- **Footnotes** on the original languages, Bible history, and Bible doctrines
- Footnotes on **difficult passages**
- **Strong's numbers** on key words in the text (NKJV / KJV / NASB / ESV)
- **Goodrick/Kohlenberger** Numbers in NIV text
- **Grammatical notations**
- Grammatical codes on **key words** in the text of the New Testament identify the forms of Greek grammar behind the English translation
- Table of **weights and measures**
- Includes **AMG's Concordance** of the Bible (KJV)

For product pricing information logon to
AMGPublishers.com

When you buy a book from **AMG Publishers**, **Living Ink Books**, or **God and Country Press**, you are helping to make disciples of Jesus Christ around the world.

How? AMG Publishers and its imprints are ministries of **AMG** (*Advancing the Ministries of the Gospel*) **International**, a non-denominational evangelical Christian mission organization ministering in over 30 countries around the world. Profits from the sale of AMG Publishers books are poured into the outreaches of AMG International.

AMG International Mission Statement

AMG exists to advance with compassion the command of Christ to evangelize and make disciples around the world through national workers and in partnership with like-minded Christians.

AMG International Vision Statement

We envision a day when everyone on earth will have at least one opportunity to hear and respond to a clear presentation of the Gospel of Jesus Christ and have the opportunity to grow as a disciple of Christ.

To learn more about AMG International and how you can pray for or financially support this ministry, please visit
www.amgmissions.org